P9-DUA-049

WINDOW CHIC

WINDOW CHIC

Illustrations by Michelle Ball
Text by Catherine Revland

HEARST BOOKS
NEW YORK

Copyright © 1994 by
s m a l l w o o d   a n d   s t e w a r t ,   i n c .

All rights reserved. No part of this book may be reproduced or utilized in any form
or by any means, electronic or mechanical, including photocopying, recording, or by
any information storage or retrieval system, without permission in writing from
the Publisher. Inquiries should be addressed to Permissions Department,
William Morrow and Company, Inc.,
1350 Avenue of the Americas, New York, N.Y. 10019.

It is the policy of William Morrow and Company, Inc., and its affiliates,
recognizing the importance of preserving what has been written, to print the books
we publish on acid-free paper, and we exert our best efforts to that end.

Library of Congress Cataloging-in-Publication Data

Ball, Michelle.
Window Chic / illustrations by Michelle Ball: text by Catherine Revland.
p. cm.
ISBN 0-688-12585-9
1. Drapery. 2. Drapery in interior decoration. I. Revland,
Catherine. II. Title.
TT390.B33 1994
746.9'4—dc20
93-21452
CIP

Printed in Singapore

First U.S. Edition
1 2 3 4 5 6 7 8 9 10

Produced by Smallwood and Stewart, Inc.
New York City

Edited by Linda Hetzer
Art-directed by Annemarie McMullan
Jacket designed by Michelle Wiener

contents

introduction

Edith Wharton, despairing over the late Victorian custom of draping windows in layers of heavy fabric that banished sunlight from the home, declared that the best window treatment was no window treatment at all. There is still a case to be made for that approach; however, the function of a window treatment is more than decorative. Needs must also be considered: for privacy, for protection from the elements, for concealing architectural features that are less than desirable, and to expand, unify, or otherwise change the perception of a room.

The window treatments presented in this book are an amalgam of the best of the past, with its love of deep folds and sumptuous fabric, and of the present, with its love of sunlight and casual simplicity. In designing a window treatment, quality of light is a major consideration. Fabric can act as a softener and diffuser of light. Colors in the sun range make light richer and warmer, and fabric with superior light-filtering qualities enhances the light. Opaque panels are best hung well outside the window frame so that when they are open the amount of light entering a room is never diminished.

Quality of fabric is another key element, and quality is not determined only by price, for some of the lowliest of cottons, like muslin gauze, make perfectly wonderful window treatments. Quality fabrics fall with softness as well as substance. They may be crisp but never stiff. Sheers are billowy and translucent, and preferably of natural fibers with their well-known light enhancing qualities. Medium-weight fabric is often lined to give it more heft and fullness, especially when the fabric is to be puddled, swagged, or caught up in a tieback. Interlining provides even more fullness; an old blanket used as interlining will make a panel an excellent sound and weather barrier. Traditional heavy draperies, of exquisite velvet, brocade, damask, tapestry, and other luxury fabrics, remain the mainstay of most drapery departments. Although yardage requirements are great, there is something to be said for investing in fabric that is to be looked at rather than sat in. And it is an investment, for these fabrics improve with age.

Yet another important quality is line. Instead of hard parallel lines, tightness, and fussy ruffles, the treatments featured here rely on the fall of the fabric, whose curves soften the architectural lines in a room. Instead of straight and symmetrical, the lines are curvilinear and serpentine. The secret is lots of fabric, generous in both width and length. When large amounts of fabric are draped and puddled or caught up in a holder, or simply hung from a rod, the most interesting things happen naturally. The way fabric is attached, with rings and tabs and casings (rather than the cumbersome attachments of old, the traverse rod and pulleys), helps the fabric fall in a way that makes a straight line graceful. These attachments allow the panels to be pulled back casually with the sweep of a hand. Striving for perfection is never the aim, for the result of that is too rigidly symmetrical, too commercial. How much more rewarding it is to loop fabric loosely over a rod and let it fall.

Instructions for duplicating the glorious window treatments shown in the watercolor renderings here, down to the smallest detail, are given in the second half of this book. An alphabetical list of terms and techniques at the end of the book contains general sewing instructions and definitions of words unique to windows and window treatments. Although the task may seem perplexing at first and the choices many, the actual measuring, cutting, sewing, and draping of fabric to create your own window treatments are by far the easiest and most rewarding tasks in home decorating.

CHAPTER ONE

window style

Style can be defined as much by what is left out as it can by what is emphasized. Eliminated are some of the less successful features of traditional window treatments: heavy cornices that block the sun, narrow pinch pleats, and that bane of finishing touches, the gathered ruffle. Instead, the fabric itself becomes the main feature: its fiber, color, pattern, weight, and width are all important. How fabric is combined with other fabrics, how it is draped, ornamented, and attached to the window, is what defines the style in the following portfolio of watercolor renderings.

a portfolio of
imaginative design ideas

 *A river valley view is framed by panels with deep bishop sleeves that seem to belong in an English castle. The fabric is ordinary cotton twill that has been lined and interlined to produce the heavy folds. A bungee cord is looped around the panels and hooked to an unseen nail. Fabric is pulled from above the cord and draped over it, producing the soft yet substantial lines of folds. Pure yellow was chosen to reflect the light of the sun as it sets over the river in the evening.*

the five-minute curtain

A border print makes an especially effective panel and valance in one. Wide fabric is needed to create these full panels, which are hung around but not over the window panes to allow for a full view of a beautiful tropical vista and to let the breeze in. The swag holders are large coat hooks around which the fabric is twisted so that the right side remains visible. The border is pulled from the swag holders and allowed to show, and the unfinished bottom edge is puddled on the floor to hide the raw edges and give shape to the treatment.

Window treatments are more theatrical and often more make-do than other facets of decorating, especially when the panels do not have to open and close. The treatments shown here require no more than five minutes to create, not counting, of course, the thorough steam pressing required for any treatment. Half the treatments open and close with the utmost simplicity: through a knotted loop, over a tieback holder, or folded double over a rod and moved by hand. No sewing is necessary when raw edges are puddled on the floor, folded back out of sight, fringed, or hemmed with iron-on fusing tape. And these lavish and often dramatic window treatments can be successfully created with fabric in the widest of price ranges, from inexpensive muslin to luxurious brocade.

A double length of very wide percale has been placed wrong sides together but not sewn, creating a reversible panel that is draped over the rod, deeply puddled, and shaped into a bishop sleeve on each side. The selvage edges are folded under at the sides. The treatment is sumptuous and also economical if you use cotton or cotton blends of a light to medium weight, especially those with a polished or embossed finish.

Nothing less than a queen-size sheet will create the luxuriously deep folds of this treatment. Solid colors are especially attractive. Here sunny yellow creates an illusion of light at a shady northern exposure. The standard queen-size top sheet allows for generous fullness in both directions: shirred tightly at the casing and draped in deep Grecian folds on the floor. New bedsheets, especially those that contain synthetic fibers, are often treated with sizing that gives the surface a crisp sheen and the folds substance and form. Old sheets can be given a medium starch after laundering and steam pressed while damp to produce a sheen. The secret to the graceful fall of the folds is the diagonal tieback, looped over the rod. The deep curve is made by pulling folds of fabric above the tassel and smoothing them not too evenly with your fingers.

The perfect solution for a temporary curtain in a vacation home requires only a length of muslin gauze and a roll of masking tape. Here the fabric is folded into gathers by hand and the underside is taped to the top of the window frame. The curtain is pulled to one side and draped loosely over a long nail hammered into the window frame.

An outsize silk scarf fits the window perfectly when it is folded in half and the top edge is slightly swagged. To take up the slack at the bottom end, the front layer is caught up in an unusual tieback that is simple to do: one end of a thin cord is tied to a ring, the other end is wrapped around a pushpin at the upper right corner. The corner of the front layer is slipped through the ring. To create an even bottom edge, a tuck is made in the top edge of the outer layer, out of sight behind the border, using a few straight pins to secure it.

An unusual approach to draping a single length of unlined fabric is to loop it tightly across the rod to form a valance that resembles ruching, an otherwise complicated form of tight gathering, in a few minutes. The panels are allowed to fall short of the floor by choice. Rustic brackets are fashioned out of driftwood nailed to the wall.

A draped valance can be used to unify more than one window. Here the sun is allowed to flow freely through open loops of a length of muslin. Any reversible fabric can be used for this no-sew valance, and the rod can be exposed as much or as little as desired, depending on the requirements for light and privacy.

A vacation home must be spruced up with the absolute minimum of effort and time. Here driftwood is tacked to the molding in lieu of a rod. Soft muslin panels have been knotted at the corners and looped through the driftwood.

This scaled-down approach to a single length of fabric draped into a panel and valance is appropriate for smaller-size windows. Here pliability of fabric is important, for unless the fabric is reversible it needs to be twisted as it is looped over the rod so the valance is right side out. Percale, polished cotton, or other fabrics with a slight sheen give the treatment the look of formality it needs when the architecture or room decor requires it.

sheers

Long out of fashion, sheers are once again popular because of their adaptability in flooding rooms with as much natural light as possible while affording privacy. Sheers have a wonderful way of filtering sunlight and reducing glare. Lace or other openwork dapples the light in a delicately beautiful way. And a transparent fabric becomes semiopaque if gathered to extra fullness, making it effective in maintaining privacy.

Many people think of sheers as a bit stiff, made of synthetic fibers, and sparsely gathered. But they don't have to be that way. New sheers, made of soft and pliable fabrics like fine cotton batiste or lawn, organdy, or chiffon, are hung with extra fullness for more privacy without reducing the amount of sunlight. Instead of a stiff line of machine hemstitching around their edges, they are given a handkerchief hem or a deep border of self-fabric, strips of

When the objective (opposite) is to frame a view of the back yard but not to see the neighbors, sheers are lightly draped over tieback holders. The sheers also serve to soften the sunset light during the dinner hour. The crowned heading helps finish off the top in a grand but scaled down way befitting the use of the ornate antique brass finials. Tieback holders are also of brass, elegantly tying together the elements of the treatment.

Every morning dawns rosy when light is filtered through pale pink lawn. The extra-wide panels are taped to the top of a mounting board that extends the height of the treatment and makes a small window look quite grand. The swag is held by a loop of ribbon that is secured to the mounting board with a pushpin, out of sight. The delightful asymmetry of the draping is accentuated with a row of staggered ball fringe trim, made by sewing together two rows of trim.

organdy, or silk ribbon. A border gives a defining edge to sheers, accentuating the undulating folds of fabric in repeated curvilinear folds. Sometimes the border is the hem itself, especially with lightweight lace or linen or finely woven cotton, when the shadow of the hem can be seen. A hem becomes a border when it is the same width on all four sides, whether it is a a narrow handkerchief hem or a deep hem several inches wide. Sheers can be crisp fabrics like fine-weave linen, organdy, or organza, or they can be soft as lingerie lace, fine batiste, or fluttery, watered silk. Although sheers are traditionally white or ecru, a sheer in a pastel color, especially a pale color in the sun range, does wonderful things to the quality of light in a room.

The new sheers do not just hang dutifully between draperies; they can also be used alone, puddled on the floor, tied back, or looped and draped.

Super soft cotton batiste is a translucent sheer that can be knotted and puddled with very satisfying results. This treatment is simple and requires no sewing. Simply drape one edge of the fabric over a rod until the bottom edge is softly puddled on the floor, then tie a loose knot in the front edge to form a valance. To conceal the raw edges on the front, lace trim, here a delicate border of wide lingerie lace, can be glued, fused, or stitched on.

Other fabric choices can range from inexpensive lightweight cotton weaves, net, chiffon, and mesh to luxurious sea island and Egyptian cottons.

A single length of antique lace is hung double to avoid having to cut it. Dress- or curtain-weight lace yardage will work equally well and may be surprisingly economical. It is also possible to create this treatment without sewing, using a glue gun to attach a row of lace trim to conceal the raw edge. The panel is slightly puddled to allow the lace to show. The front layer is lightly draped over a tieback holder, hidden under folds of lace.

The luxury range of sheers includes fine silk, cotton lawn, handkerchief linen, or the silk georgette used here, especially feasible when the yardage requirements are low. Two yards of forty-five-inch-wide georgette are sufficient for these curtains, for extra full-ness is not needed when a fabric already has substance. The heading has been fused with a one-inch band of silk ribbon. This also reinforces the point at which the fabric is caught up in the clip-on rings. The highly visible edges are finished with a neat and narrow handkerchief hem.

Borders frame sheers in a most attractive way, and also serve the practical purpose of hiding seams and seam allowances, an important consideration when hanging see-through fab-ric. The band can be made of ribbon trim, but here it is a bias strip of the same fabric used to slipcover the couch.

Ordinary synthetic sheers, especially white ones, can be made to look very elegant indeed, as long as the fabric falls softly and does not have a shiny surface. Puddling gives a look of weight to an otherwise insubstantial flow of fabric. The deep curve of the valance allows the wonderful sunburst molding of the half-round window to show.

panels

Traditional does not have to mean staid or boring. The traditional panel can be modified in a variety of ways. Many of the panels shown here have such an elegant look that you may assume they are too expensive to consider. Not so. Treating inexpensive fabrics with extra fullness creates a look of richness. Instead of pinch pleats and a traverse rod, these panels have rings or tabs at the heading and are opened and closed easily. Rods are placed above and to the side of the window frame, especially with heavier fabrics, to allow for maximum light.

Some panels do not have to be full to be beautiful. Sometimes they look best hung with minimal fullness or none at all, like a shade, especially when there is an attractive pattern to display. And the panel edges, rather than being a distraction, become an attractive design feature. They are given borders, from a narrow handkerchief hem to a wide strip of organdy, on all four sides. Of equal width, the borders become a decorative frame for the panel. Some of the panels require only minimal sewing; none of them requires more than a few hours to create.

Sometimes two panels (opposite) can frame an entire wall, especially when they have generous proportions like these unlined lightweight linen curtains with handkerchief hems. Long tabs allow them to brush the floor even when they are held back by the antique glass tieback holders. The brass rod and finials match the picture frame, uniting the elements across the wall.

This highly formalized use of two fabrics is actually a tribute to asymmetry, the print interspersed with a flowing river of satin lining. The folds of the draping are evened out by hand, but not too precisely. The lining is in the sunset range of coral-to-bronze, which beautifully reflects the light from the outside.

The soft, deep and flowing folds of the box pleat are a welcome relief from the tiny pinch pleats of conventional drapery panels. Double fullness is the secret to this deeply pleated panel, of medium-weight silk and cotton damask lined and interlined with an old flannel blanket to create maximum weight as well as to serve as a barrier to the cold. The box pleats are four inches deep on each side, making the entire panel a double thickness. The many layers of panel, interlining, and lining are topstitched together in parallel lines at the heading, creating deep inverted goblet pleats whose undulating folds are enhanced by puddling the fabric on the floor.

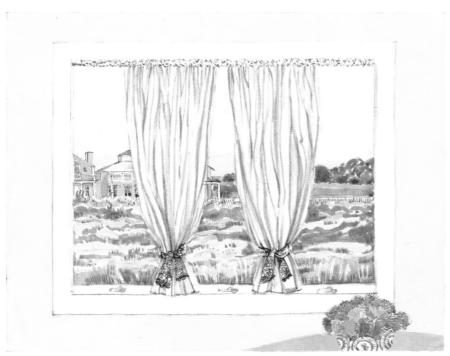

An unconventional yet highly pleasing treatment of a casement window with two vertical mullions has panels that conceal the mullions but leave the sides of the window unadorned. The ruching on the rod and the casing on the panels are the same contrasting fabric, and triple fullness is used in both ruching and panel so they appear to be all one piece. Lacy embroidered scarves are used as tiebacks and are attached to the window frame.

Coordinating fringe sewn between two layers of chintz accentuates the repeated loops of this simple drape and valance. Sumptuous in proportion and line, this treatment has the added weight of two layers of fabric. Sewing two lengths of the same fabric back to back allows for great freedom in creating the drape because the right side of the fabric is always showing. Ornate pineapple finials are displayed to good advantage when contrasted with the simplicity of the draping.

25

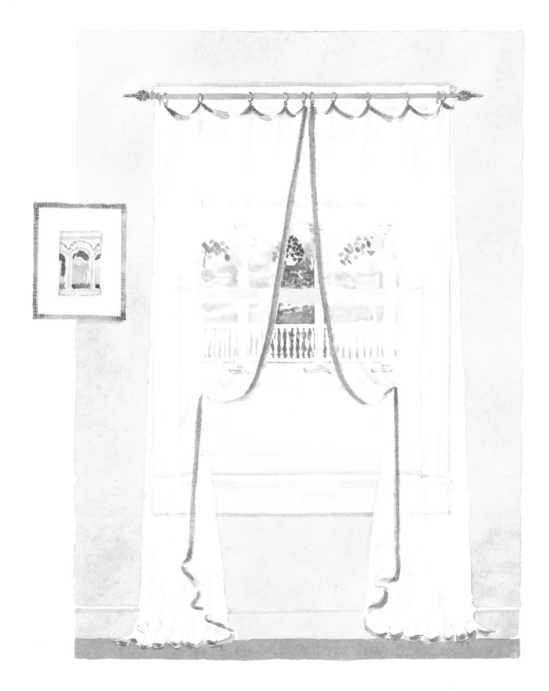

What could be more gracious than crisp silk organza curtains with a ribbon border of silk satin? Here a pair of panels frames a porch window where the fabric is protected from the direct rays of the sun. Silk crepe, organza, georgette, and some synthetic blends have a luscious way of flowing, and the price per yard is not necessarily high. The curving lines of the folds created by the tiebacks, which are attached to the innermost frame of the window, are accentuated by the silk band. The same band creates a border on all four sides of the panels and at the heading also serves as reinforcement for the rings.

Dress-weight lace yardage is more pliable and lightweight than curtain-weight lace, and produces a billowy panel that is close to a sheer in delicacy. The highly visible raw edges are finished with a handkerchief hem that forms a one-inch band on all four sides. The edges are folded under twice and neatly mitered at the corners to form an attractive edge that gives a little weight to the corners, anchoring them when the panel floats in a breeze, and makes the treatment completely reversible. Iron-on fusing tape makes this a simple job that requires no sewing.

Tabs are another simplified and stylish alternative to the traditional pinch pleat. Cut a couple of inches deeper than the rod, they open and shut easily and can be lengthened to allow the fabric to reach the floor. Here the tabs are cut with the stripe running down the center and aligned with the stripe in the panel. Cool green and white sailcloth, treated with minimal fullness to show off the stripe, acts as a shade for a bright southern exposure.

A lining in the sun color range, here a brilliant yellow moire, shows a spectacular use of a contrasting color both inside and outside the window. The panel is hung like a shade with no fullness, the best way to display to full advantage this beautiful Florentine print. The triangle of solid color is achieved by securing the corner with a pin attached to the lining side. The underside of the panel is taped to the top of the window frame, making the attachment stationary; the curtain masks a view of a brick wall and a neighbor's window.

The wide organdy border on all four edges of this batiste curtain defines and gives weight to the edges. Seam allowances can be seen through such lightweight fabric; here they are trimmed to one-quarter inch and neatly concealed under the strips of organdy, which are fused with iron-on tape to produce a seamless border. The corners are mitered and fused as well, so that the only sewing required is attaching the small white plastic rings to the heading. By sewing them to the bottom edge of the organdy, a self-valance is created.

A simple casing with crown makes for easy installation of these light cotton batiste panels with self-tiebacks. The fabric is sheer enough to be used in a low-light room yet opaque enough to afford privacy. The edge of the fabric is draped loosely over a nail or pushpin and is easily detached for closing. The point at which the edge is pulled back depends on the height of the window, but one-third the length of the panel from the floor balances this treatment. The fabric is puddled romantically on the floor, creating soft folds that add to the sumptuous look.

A double length of lace curtain yardage with a finished border is quickly draped over a rod and knotted. The raw edges can be puddled, or lace edging can be glued, fused, or sewn on to finish them. This dramatic and graceful use of lace by the yard is devoid of the fussy or overdone look that long expanses of lace can sometimes have. Two lace panels can also be used, sewn together at the headings with the seam taped to the back of the rod, out of sight.

Somewhere between a shade and a valance, this stunning fabric is caught up in a bow with loops of drapery tape. The top is hung on an inside-mounting rod. Although this treatment is stationary, a shade that can be raised and lowered can be made by cutting the panel longer and sewing snaps or Velcro to the ends of the tape, and slip stitching ornamental bows to the tape.

The welted hem gives an elegant finishing touch to any weight of fabric, acting the role of the lead drapery weights that are often sewn into the hems of traditional drapery panels. Welting is especially effective with stripes or plaids, when the casing strips are cut on the bias. Welting is also a solution in repairing vintage panels, whose hems often become threadbare along the bottom fold. A casing strip is created from the hem by cutting along the fold, and the frayed bottom edge is given new substance without sacrificing an inch of length.

one window three ways

This is the traditional draw drape in all its splendor, hung on a rod of grand proportions with equally grand finials. The panels fall to the floor in the rich, deep folds of a Renaissance painting. Such a luxurious effect is achieved by puddling an extra twelve inches of fabric on the floor and attaching heavy wooden rings to box pleats that are a full eight inches across. Additional heaviness is created with a flannel interlining, a good way to recycle an old blanket or sheet. Although the statement is sumptuous, the cost does not have to be. Fabric can be cotton duck or brushed denim, as long as the color is rich and deep.

A window treatment is a versatile and simple way to make a design statement that incorporates all the elements in a room. It can accent, complement, or play tricks with the eye, concealing or amplifying, depending upon the effect the home designer wants to achieve.

In order to make a statement, the window treatment must be defined in terms of details. If romantic, how romantic? With frills and bows or in the simple softening of a line created by puddling? If formal, how formal? With tailored simplicity but without making a room look uninviting and museum-like? The three illustrations shown here are quite different in look and feel, but all make design statements that speak well of a room, defining the traditional approach made simple, emphasizing the elements of line and color, and elevating the importance of the pliability and weight of the fabric.

Romancing a room does not have to include lace and ruffles. For those who prefer a streamlined look even in a romantic setting, a sedate stripe, a medium-weight fabric unlined for a light and airy look, is gently gathered and tied with bows. The rod is positioned a full twelve inches above the window frame so the eye is fooled into thinking the space is larger than it actually is. Long tabs have been used to allow the panels to reach the floor when untied, and barely skim it when the bows are in place.

If light needs to be diffused, lace is a great favorite, filtering out the glare and creating a dappled effect through a filigree of fine thread. Here two lace panels are used for extra fullness and are tied back to one side with a narrow ribbon to create a deeply curved line. The top of the panels has a casing with a scallop-bordered crown.

A vintage lace tablecloth can be cut in half crosswise to produce two sensational shorter curtains or cafes, particularly if the design has a central medallion.

valances

A grandmother's embroidered linen tablecloth has been folded in half over a rod, creating a reversible window treatment. The swag and tails are formed with bands of drapery tape encircling the fabric and attached with pushpins to the window frame, out of sight. Linen tablecloths are especially adaptable because of their heavy crispness and the great light-filtering qualities of the fabric. If there is trim at the hems, the underlayer of the tablecloth can be pulled down an inch to create a double border to the bottom edge.

Aesthetically, valances finish off the top edge of a window treatment or are used alone. Practically, valances conceal the hardware and attachments or the wall above an extended rod. The demands of practicality may determine the aesthetic choices, but in this section is a great wealth of possible styles.

Structurally, there are two kinds of valances: those that are attached to a rod by casings, rings, or other methods and are sewn and hung like very short curtains, and valances that are draped over a rod or swag holders. Deep curves in valances are created by cutting or swagging or sometimes both; shaped valances create a graceful concave inner curve. When swagged, valances can have tails that extend as low as the sill or even all the way to the floor. Valances usually need to be lined because their wrong sides are often visible.

The traditional approach to valances tends to be very fussy, with cornices, pelmets, and jabots. Here the approach is much simpler; cutting a diagonal line and making a casing produces a deliciously undulating inner edge with no need to measure, mark, piece, or pleat.

A valance and swag has been made from a scrap of awning-stripe fabric, its ends cut on a sharp diagonal to create the long undulating tails. Lining is necessary because of the way the fabric folds back on itself. This treatment looks best with a contrasting lining that shows off the diagonal folds to full advantage. The rod has been extended to unify the ensemble of window and pictures and to make a lone window on a wall look more substantial.

This stylish solution to the problem of what to do with unmatched panels also conceals the fact that the panels are too short for the window. By using them as a valance the two colors are blended, making an interesting pattern. The panels are drawn tightly in the middle of the rod and then looped over the corner hardware to create the look of a swag and tail.

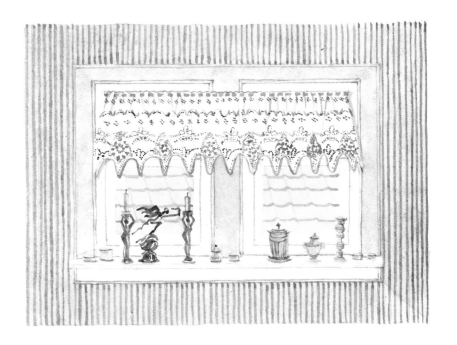

The deeply scalloped edge of a needlework piece makes for a striking valance that reaches to eye level on these windows. This elaborately worked piece of vintage cutwork embroidery was an undamaged side of a frayed tablecloth bought at a yard sale. The side was cut two inches from the innermost row of embroidered eyelet and folded under to become a faced heading. A slim rod was threaded through the cutwork.

A semicircle of fabric the width of the window is gathered off-center, using a line of hand gathers, and the edges are trimmed with heavy fringe and tassels, like those on a damask piano shawl. In an elegant room with a few period touches, such a valance becomes a high Victorian tour de force .

A fine wool shawl with a richly colored challis lining is a natural for a simple valance and swag, for both sides contribute to the effect and the treatment is appealing from inside and out. The shawl is draped over the rod a few inches off center to create asymmetrical tails. The swag is taped on the underside to secure it to the rod.

This valance pulls out all the stops to frame magnificently a view of a city on a hill. Two sizes of tieback holders, the larger one elevated to reign over the treatment like the center jewel in a crown, are used. Sturdy holders are needed to support the heavy upholstery-weight fabric. Plush, velvet, and even heavy canvas are all suited to this treatment that is panel, valance, and swag all in one. The less arranging of the heavy fabric the better; just center the length over the center tieback and let it rest on the corner holders before letting it fall regally and deeply puddled to the floor.

tiebacks

Tiebacks are a most harmonious marriage of form and function. They allow for maximum light in the room while transforming the straight lines of a panel or curtain into graceful curves. The fullness of those curves depends on how much of the fabric is pulled loose above the tieback.

And where the tieback is placed ~ as high as the first mullion, as low as the apron, off to one side, or in the center ~ depends on many factors, including the view out the window, the need for privacy, and the amount of light desired. Where tiebacks are placed can completely change the look of a window treat-

Center tiebacks (opposite) look best with extra full panels. These rustic kettle cloth curtains have a multiple loop of ordinary rope holding them together in a somewhat permanent tieback creating a treatment that works like a shade for a bright southern exposure.

Tiebacks can be simply a length of dress-weight or more expensive drapery-weight cable cord tied into a loop and hung over the rod, eliminating the need for nailing into the wall or window frame. Focal points can often help determine the placement of a tieback; here the choice was made to draw attention to the horizon with its spectacular peaks and valleys. The dress-weight cable cord has been looped double to look more substantial. To create extra fullness, two double bedsheets have been used, their top hems threaded through the rod and gathered tightly to create a shirred heading.

ment. Try tiebacks in several different places before you make a final decision on placement.

Tiebacks can be made of narrow bands that match the panel fabric, of contrasting luxury fabric, or of ordinary twine or cord. They can also be as simple as a gathered line of diagonal stitches or a tiny plastic ring stitched to the panel and slipped over a cup hook. Tiebacks can be used succesfully on the heaviest as well as the thinnest of fabrics. There is no simpler or more successful way to introduce the curved line into a window treatment or to soften the angular lines of a room than with a tieback.

Bishop sleeves are created by pulling fabric up and poufing it above a tieback, which then disappears beneath the folds.

Here both sides of the panel are poufed to produce a full bishop sleeve. The graceful goblet lines are accentuated by drawing the rings closely

together. Expensive cable cord and tassels are used only as decoration; ordinary butcher's cord, hidden in the folds, actually holds up the fabric.

Tightly shirred tissue-thin voile is caught up at apron level with strands of pearls wound double and secured to small nails. Lightweight lawn, gauze, or very soft cottons will not create bulk at the hems, so are perfect for this unique approach to tiebacks.

Tiebacks can be coordinated with tabs for a unifying effect. Double lengths of cable cord have been sewn into the heading to form sturdy tabs for these heavy box-pleated panels. The matching tiebacks have rings sewn on the ends, to attach to a cup hook, making them easily detachable when the drapes are drawn every evening and pulled back every morning. Folded bands of fabric, ribbon, or other sturdy trim that is finished on all sides can also be used as coordinating tiebacks and tabs as long as they will support the weight of the panel.

As soon as a length of fabric is caught up in a tieback and lifted slightly, interesting fold lines are created. The fullness of the panels adds much to that interest. This self-fabric tieback is simply a folded strip, unsewn, that is tacked to the window frame. The inner edge of the tieback is placed at the first mullion to accentuate the height ~ as does the extended rod placement ~ of this majestic treatment of an equally majestic view.

Three long scarves (top left), one patterned and two solid, are braided to form this amply rounded tieback. Strips of fabric can also be used, folded so that the raw edges are concealed within the braid.

This temporary garland tieback (top right) is made by poking fresh leaves, buds, vines, or flowers into a wire tieback. Choose flora that won't wilt before the party is over; bay laurel, holly, and broadleaf evergreens will last through a holiday season.

This softly petaled satin rose (center), made of expensive bridal-weight silk satin, needs a mere eighteen inches of the wonderful, buttery soft fabric for both the tieback band and the rose. Complete instructions for this tieback and the tassel below are on pages 108–109.

The knotted tieback (bottom left) is simple yet stylish. Here, medium-weight fabric produces this substantial knot, which can be tied in a casually tightened loop as shown, or tied so the knot forms a horizontal band of fabric.

A drapery tassel of substance and heft (bottom right) can be made by rolling a nine-inch length of tricolored drapery fringe and securing it tightly. A double layer of dress-weight cable cord is used for the tieback, picking up one of the three colors in the tassel.

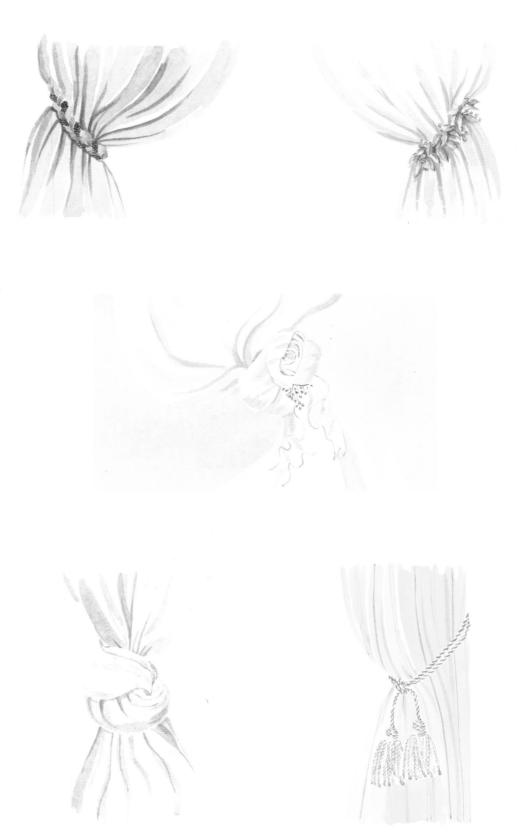

two fabrics

The simplest use of two fabrics is to hang the panels and sheers on a single rod. Here they open and close on small wooden rings. Instead of a separate rod for a valance, the sheers are folded over to become a self-valance. Unless the fabric in the panels is reversible, the valance is cut along the fold and sewn to the panel so that the right side faces out. Two windows can also be treated as one and extended upward. The depth of the valance will conceal the wall between the top of the window and the rod and create a unifying border along the wall between them.

There are many reasons for using two different fabrics at a window, among them to create extra fullness, to allow panels to be draped over a rod, to use only one rod, and to make the treatment finished both inside and out. There is only one requirement for the outcome ~ a pleasing unity. Pairing up colors is most often the simplest way to combine two fabrics. Select two shades from the room decor and see how they complement each other with the sun behind them. Combinations can produce dramatic and unexpected outcomes, like a chemical equation, and can sometimes be quite sur-

prising: a stripe that frames a print or solid, the combination of velvet and taffeta that creates interest in both texture and hue, or a sheer and an opaque fabric that produce an interesting play of light. Marrying two patterns is not quite so simple a task, unless it is a floral and a stripe, which can be used diagonally to great effect. Two prints with a different background color can be used together most pleasingly, as long as there is a difference in scale. One combination that works especially well is that of a large scale floral with central motifs and a medium or small scale floral with an overall pattern.

Two sets of single sheets are used to maximum effect in a treatment that looks equally attractive from the outside as the inside. Rings are used so that the treatment can be opened and closed with ease at French doors, providing ready access to the patio. A large-scale pattern can often hold its own better than a small one when combined with a stripe. Cool blue was chosen for the backdrop to tone down the tropical sunlight of a south-west window, yet the combination creates a mood that is light and breezy. The rings are widely placed to create extra-deep folds, and the lining is folded under to form a capped valance as well as a deep border on the sides. The rod has been attached six inches above the window to make use of the full length of the bedsheets.

A pair of vintage panels in peach velvet is used with newly purchased velvet in a toned down taupe, a shade richly colored fabric often achieves with age. A length of taupe velvet is cut in half and hung on the inside of the vintage panels giving them additional fullness and weight. The taupe velvet makes a generous swagged valance that together with the panels frames a right-angled urban view with voluptuously undulating curves.

A ground-floor win-
dow treatment is
often almost as visi-
ble from the outside as from
within. Here a pattern with
an interesting geometric print
beautifully frames the solid
sunny yellow curtains. The
wide border creates a high
crown above the casing and
outlines all the other edges.
Medium-weight fabric is ideal
for this treatment. However,
whichever fabrics you choose
should be similar in weight to
make for ease in stitching and
compatibility in draping.

The vintage shades of ruby and pale gold become even richer and more interesting when combined. The extra fullness of the panels creates a tight gathering on the rod called ruching, framing the top sumptuously. Such richness requires embellishments to match, here heavy cable cord, tassels, and fringe along the edges. The rod has been placed on a mounting board that is extended to just below the ceiling molding, which makes the living-room ceiling look higher than it really is. Although the approach is English in its use of heavy fabric, the traditional valance is eliminated altogether, and the panels are lightly but gracefully tied back to create a scaled-down version of traditional formality that is more appropriate to a modern lifestyle.

A sedate brocade is lined with an exciting stripe of pink and yellow moire that unfolds like a banner when the curtains are tied back to the wall. Stripes look especially pleasing when draped or cut on the diagonal. An embossed solid is easily and successfully combined with a print and, in this case, both fabrics are also used on furnishings in the room. The panels are extra full, forming a deep ruching on the rod, a finishing touch that eliminates the need for a valance.

multiple windows

Treating more than one window in a room can create a dilemma ~ should they be treated individually, or separately but in relation to each other? And what about the bare wall between the windows? The answers depend on how the windows relate to the room and the view they frame. Perhaps no aspect of window treatment is so difficult to convey in words as the relationship of one window to another, and together their relationship to the room, for the variables are too great. These illustrations show the wide diversity of window placement and the challenges they present.

A minimal but spectacular approach to treating a trio of small windows is to hang panels with a beautiful motif such as the intricate eyelet cutwork illustrated here. Recessed rods allow the molding to show, further unifying the treatment. The cutwork panels barely cover the window panes and seem to float on their slender rods.

50

Here a transom-like window over French doors, an example of a "what do you do with it?" window, is treated as one window with the treatment extending to the ceiling. Despite the elegant look, the fabric is quite ordinary. A single length of inexpensive cotton or cotton blend is swagged over a pair of decorative tiebacks and deeply puddled on the floor, requiring no sewing and not even a rod. In a room with high ceilings this creates a dramatic, even theatrical effect. That such luxury is available at a few dollars a yard is great motivation for creating one's own window treatments.

51

One solution to treating the bare wall between windows is to use a mounting board, here extended from corner to corner and topped with a piece of decorative molding that has been painted to match the window frame. The panels and valance are tacked to the bottom underside of the board, which crowns the entire wall.

Lace yardage with a scalloped edge lends itself economically to creating the valance, which is cut lengthwise along the scalloped selvage edge.

Treating three windows with tieback curtains (left) achieves a look of pleasing formality by placing all three in the same direction and using borders. The silk ribbon creates graceful lines that flow into each other. The tiebacks are simply small tassels attached with pushpins.

Versatile sheers can treat not just a single window (below) but an entire wall gracefully. Here light is emphasized by using sheers like heavy drapery in an old-fashioned panel and swag. The asymmetry is carefully planned: the bottom edge of the inside of the panel on each window drops just to the height of the fireplace.

one picture window three ways

Deep box pleats fastened to rings are a simple and attractive alternative to pinch-pleated drapery on a traverse rod, and more soft and flowing as well. This treatment is unusual in two ways. Not only is it hung on short rods, eliminating the problem of what to do with the exposed rod between the windows when there is no valance, it also boldly combines two prints, which meet at sill level, gracefully incorporating the lines of the drape with the lines of the window frame.

The treatment of a picture window has posed a problem since the window first became popular after World War II. Yet this oversized window has remained a favorite over the years because of the way it floods a room with sunshine and gives generous display to a beautiful view. But how do you treat it without resorting to high-tech attachments and the ubiquitous pinch pleat? These illustrations answer that question with simple, straightforward elegance. The picture window is a dramatically pleasing place to display a favorite fabric with extra fullness and a softened line, hung to the floor, for the extra width of the window almost demands the length to achieve balance.

A more formal and dramatic approach uses a single length of fabric looped once over a rod and allowed to flow voluminously onto the floor. Yet all this elegance can be achieved with a modest fabric such as percale or polished cotton, which can be interlined to give extra body and fullness to the folds. A self-lined fabric will allow both sides of the drape to be exposed, creating a completely reversible treatment.

A light and airy approach to framing a rustic view employs traditional lace panels and a full shaped valance that crowns the window and allows for the maximum amount of filtered sunlight. The scalloped border of the lace curtain yardage is cut in strips and used to edge the hems of both panels and valance to unify them.

cafe curtains

This cafe treatment of a ground-floor window successfully breaks the rules in two ways: rather than be concerned with where the rod crosses the mullion, the decision of placement was made for reasons of privacy and the design feature in the curtain. Shortening the panel would have destroyed the balance. Instead, the valance is shortened, creating a pleasing balance in the treatment as a whole. Although the two patterns do not match in color or design, nevertheless they complement each other and provide an interesting contrast in a simple, scaled-down room.

The use of the cafe curtain has expanded well beyond its origins in restaurants, where it allowed diners to view the passing scene while being shielded from the eyes of passersby. Cafes remain a stylish and time-honored way to treat the bottom half of a window. Cafe curtains without valances afford maximum light and best display a beautiful view. Valances can be used to expand the height of a treatment or to soften the sun's glare without interfering with the view. With or without a valance, this simple way to hang a movable curtain remains a perennial favorite. And there are no hard-and-fast rules to follow. Rods can be hung above and below the sash, at a mullion, or in between, wherever it is most pleasing. As a result, the cafe is the most adaptable of curtains as well as the simplest to sew, the ideal way to use up a remnant or vintage fabric that is too short for a sill-length curtain.

Each tier of this versatile cafe can be opened or closed as each is hung on its own rod, increasing the options for adjusting the light. The top layer, finished with a casing with a high crown, becomes the valance. Other layers have casings without crowns that are concealed behind the overlapping hemlines when closed. This treatment is an ideal way to use very narrow fabric yardage or remnants. Use inside mounted rods or tension rods so that the molding around the window serves as a frame for the tiers.

A recessed window is always a pleasing frame for a cafe, especially when crowned with a swagged valance. For the valance, the full width of the fabric has been used with the design motif centered in the middle of each valance. The edges of the tails are cut straight across but could also be cut on a slight diagonal. The valance is taped to the top of the molding and the swag is created with an unseen loop of self-fabric secured with a push-pin into the molding. The grosgrain bows are made separately and pinned to the tieback.

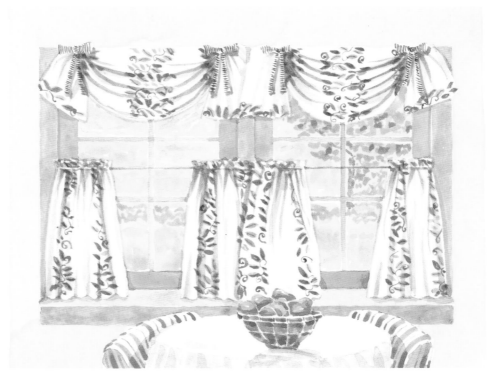

found objects

Any attractive piece of fabric that is pliable and has finished edges can be instantly transformed into a window treatment. A found object to be used alone should be no smaller than an inch or two shorter than the window and at least one-fifth the length of the finished drop. Anything smaller will look skimpy. However, many found objects can also be hung grouped together. Especially effective are pieces with deep worked edges, as the overlapping scallops or points form a decorative border. Nonfabric objects, like paper, a collection of glass bottles, or rows of plants on glass shelves, can also be used. Whatever the choice, the pleasure of a found object as window treatment comes from the fact that its original use was for something else. The most successful found object as window treatment is one that is readily converted and has qualities that are enhanced by sunlight.

The vivid and cheerful colors of a serape (opposite) plus its generous length make it an excellent found object for a curtain, especially in a child's room where bright colors are always appreciated. Here the narrowness of the fabric is not a drawback, and the tails end in a long and wonderful fringe.

Square tablecloths, especially those with a stripe or plaid, often work best folded diagonally over a rod to become a pointed valance. The width of the treatment is adjusted by folding the tablecloth slightly off center. A wider fabric can be given a little fullness if pulled in slight gathers across the rod. The tablecloths are paired with crisp linen for the cafes. Take the tablecloth with you when you shop for the cafe fabric so you can match not only the color but also the weight of the fabric.

Found objects too small to work alone can often be used in a series, like this collection of vintage neckties. Here, the neckties overlap slightly to produce a zigzag edge. The narrow end of the tie has been looped over the rod under the wider end and tucked out of sight. Crocheted doilies, placemats, pennants, or other small fabric objects with a finished edge can also be effective.

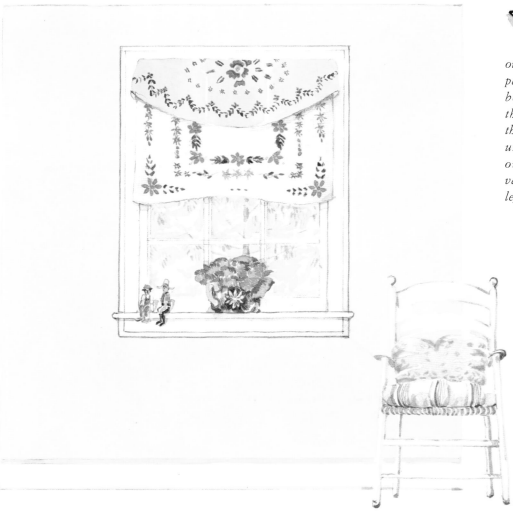

Two small tea cloths from the 1940s, one square and the other oval, with different colors and patterns, work well together because they are both from the same period. Ovals lend themselves very well to being used as valances, and large ovals can become swagged valances with enough fabric left over to form tails.

A collection of unusual and colorful tea towels creates an eye-catching valance for a soft fall of batiste sheers. The sides of the towels can be folded in to adjust the overall width of the treatment and to display the designs to their full advantage. The lengths of the towels vary slightly to add further interest.

Pieces of vintage lace or needlework like this monogrammed cutwork linen dresser scarf are often easily converted into window treatments, especially those with a border on all four sides and a central motif. The runner's dimensions fall just short of the frame, and it is hung flat like a tapestry with a uniform space on all four sides. The top border is folded over and threaded with picture-hanging wire. This minimal treatment makes the dresser scarf seem to float at the window for its thin strand of wire wound around small cup hooks is all but invisible.

Tablecloths with borders have an extra boon, for the borders define the edges and fall in graceful folds, especially when hung diagonally. Due to its generous proportions and the size of the window, this tablecloth forms a self-valance with its own border, and the excess fabric has been eased to the sides and folded to create undulating tails. Larger tablecloths can reach all the way to the floor.

This eight-foot-long embroidered linen banquet tablecloth, is a coffee-stained flea market find bleached to a snow white. To avoid having to shorten it, the tablecloth has been draped across the rod and used as a valance, keeping the integrity of the design and the borders intact. Any treasured heirloom tablecloth too valuable to be constantly laundered can be enjoyed as a window treatment.

Their finished hems and facing make bed-sheets the perfect found object for a window treatment. All that is necessary is a good pressing. The top hem of the sheet becomes the casing; you can clip the stitches on the edges if necessary. Here a child's bedsheet is knotted so that a favorite color is centered in a motif in the knot.

Window treatments need not be limited to fabric. White parchment or heavyweight butcher paper, pleated accordian style and stenciled, is used as an attractive horizontal curtain shade. To avoid wear and tear on the paper make the curtain stationary by cutting it to the size you want for privacy and to let in a comfortable amount of light. To make grommets, punch small holes with a hole puncher and make them sturdier with cloth reinforcement rings.

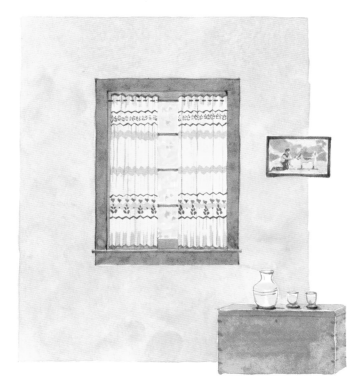

Any group of found objects can be a candidate for a window treatment, the only requirement being practicality, ease of installation, and a visually pleasing end result. Here glass shelves are attached inside a tall and narrow window with southern exposure in a plant lover's apartment. The marriage of necessity and aesthetics is most successful. The four shelves are placed far enough apart to avoid shading the plants below, and at varying heights. The climbing vine will eventually form a graceful frame around the window.

adjustments

A pair of narrow floral print panels is used with sheers of the same background color of pale pink to expand a single window treatment to cover two windows in a new home. The valance has been made into throw pillows for the couch, pleasingly blending the elements of the decor. This treatment is also a way to save money when buying yardage, especially when two lengths per window would make the window treatment too costly.

When a couch or chair move from house to house, nothing is required to make the change but a strong back. The same can rarely be said of a window treatment, due to the great difference in size and placement of windows. Fortunately, there are many ways to reuse window treatents that do not require cutting into the fabric. To shorten, hems can be double and even triple rolled, the extra bulk improving the look of heavy drapery. Tucks can be taken above the hem or below the heading, or the heading can be folded over to become a valance. The height of rods can be adjusted to accommodate the existing length of the panel, or the excess can be puddled on the floor. Lengthening often requires additional contrasting fabric, either as yardage or as trim. A row of welting on the bottom can finish off a let-down hem, providing the additional inches needed to reach the floor. Swagging a length of fabric to create a valance is another way to scrimp on length, allowing the rod to be lowered. And the use of two or more swag holders allows you to piece and still have the look of one continuous flow of fabric. In the sewing section and in Terms and Techniques complete instructions are given for piecing, tucking, and other techniques used to lengthen or shorten existing window treatments.

A move out of the family home into a retirement community or to a dream cottage by a lake often means making drapes from a long parlor window fit a smaller window. Here to make use of the extra length, the rod is placed well above the top of the window and a self-valance is created without cutting into the fabric because the woven plaid is reversible. Rings are sewn on at the fold line. Finials screwed into the window frame are used as tieback holders.

Drapes from a former home can be made to fit the windows of a high-ceilinged Victorian house. These pale blue draperies were lengthened a full eighteen inches with an insert of blue and white silk chintz, allowing them to be deeply puddled on the floor. Additional fabric for tiebacks makes effective use of a small amount of luxury cloth and further unifies the treatment. Inserts can be made of lace, brocade, a border print, velvet, or taffeta, depending on the weight of the existing panel. The expense of fine fabric for the insert is minimal when you need less than a yard.

embellishments

A double row of light-weight ball fringe gives substance to the inside edges of a diagonally cut valance, emphasizing the graceful undulating lines created when solid fabric with checked lining is swagged. The second row of trim is sewn so that the ball fringe is staggered.

Substance is the key to successful embellishments. Trim provides weight as well as texture and adornment to the edges of a window treatment, defining, shaping, and emphasizing the flowing lines of fabric. When simplicity is the goal, a window treatment often needs an attractive edging as a unifying framework as well as for the practical purpose of hiding seam lines. Trim looks particularly attractive with combinations of fabric or reversible treatments with contrasting linings. Because the yardage requirements for window treatment trim are significant, expensive drapery-weight trim may be out of the question. Fortunately, there are stunning ways to economize.

*Trim with scalloped or worked edges
beautifully defines the seams of a draped panel.*

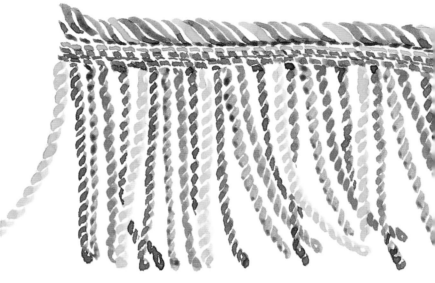

*An ornate tassel finishes off
a cable cord tieback with high style.*

*A lavish multicolored drapery-weight fringe with twisted
cable cord provides an elegant border to plain and simple fabrics.*

*Drapery tape comes in a myriad of colors,
textures, and patterns.*

*Wide embroidered ribbon makes an
especially attractive border, neatly mitered at the corners.*

*A double row of staggered dress-weight fringe is substantial
enough for trimming curtains and drapes.*

CHAPTER TWO

all about fabric

No other feature in home design requires the number of yards of fabric as a room with several windows treated in full, floor-length panels. Your choice of fabric is the most critical decision in creating a window treatment. Before buying many yards of cloth, bring home a yard or two and live with it for a while. Drape it over a window to see how it filters light throughout the day, including a cloudy day, and how it looks at night. See how it relates to the overall decorating scheme of the room. Remember, you want to be absolutely sure not only that you like your choice, but that you love it.

A length of chintz with a fabulous print is hung on a rod without gathering, like a flag unfurled, all the better to display the pattern to its fullest glory. Such a minimal use of fabric ~ it barely reaches the sill ~ is a stylish solution for expensive cloth. This medium-weight chintz requires no lining because it has substantial body. However, an inexpensive fabric with a spectacular print can also be used by lining it with cotton muslin to give it the extra body it needs.

pliability

The most important consideration in choosing fabric for window treatments is how it flows. Some heavy fabric is too stiff or lifeless to be successfully draped or to fall gracefully in pleats or gathers. Some lightweight fabric can hang like a limp dish towel rather than flutter in a breeze. With any fabric, the qualities to look for are pliability and substance, and this requires a hands-on approach. Feel the fabric between your fingers, and when you find one you like, unfold a yard or two and let it fall from the bolt to see how it flows. Gather a bunch of it in your hand to see how it falls in folds.

filtering light

The second consideration in selecting fabric for a window treatment is how it diffuses light. Lace, fine cotton, linen, and sheers are perennial favorites because of the way they dapple and soften sunlight. Unlined, these natural fibers enhance the quality of sunlight filtered through the curtain. Unlike synthetic fabrics, which reflect light, natural fibers absorb it and take out the harshness.

weather

Fabric at a window may not receive the kind of wear and tear that furnishings get, but it is constantly exposed to the elements, and how much sun the fabric will receive as well as how much of a barrier to sound, dust, soot, cold, and wind the curtain must

A swagged valance needs no hardware; the back of the fabric is taped to the top molding. Trim wound twice and anchored with a pushpin is used as a swag holder.

Stripes are especially effective across the top of a window that displays a collection of plants or glass bottles because the valance acts as a frame for the display.

provide is a primary consideration in the selection of a fabric. You can line fragile fabrics to forestall disintegration in full sunlight and richly colored ones to prevent fading as well as to make the treatments more of a barrier to the elements.

color and pattern

Because fabric at a window may have the sun behind it much of the time, light is also an important factor in color choice. The color of the window treatment helps determine the mood in a room. On a cloudy day or at night, even a pale shade in the sun color range creates an illusion of sunlight. In fact, these colors intensify in hue at night or on cloudy days and pale out when the sun shines directly on them.

The range of sun colors is very broad ~ from the palest ivory and yellow to rose, coral, and salmon, then deepening to the sunset colors of gold, bronze, ruby, and purple. All these shades will enhance a window treatment's light-filtering qualities inside a room. Lined in sun colors, the window treatment also looks beautiful from where it is seen by the most people ~ from the outside. In a room with too much natural light, a blue or green fabric at the window will help cool it down.

Select patterns for a window treatment on the basis of scale and how they complement other patterns used in the room. When many yards of fabric are required, avoid small-scale patterns. They can be used in a kitchen or for a country feeling, but are inappropriate for more formal decor.

Striped fabric can often be used successfully in a window treatment, particularly when a band of the fabric cut on the bias is attached on all four sides, defining the panel with an attractive border. Large-scale patterns with central motifs can be used very effectively in a window treatment, especially one whose panels fall to the floor. When other fabric in a room is of a solid color, particularly on the neutral side, a window treatment with a distinctive pattern can become a stunning display of both color and pattern creating a design feature in the room without overwhelming it.

Be careful of using many yards of fabric with a large-scale pattern or vivid color in a room already full of both. Remember that the scale of a window treatment can quickly destroy the balance and harmony of a room's overall decor when multiple yards of fabric are used with a heavy hand.

fabric weights

The weight of a fabric will have direct bearing on whether it is used in a window treatment as a sheer, a curtain, or a panel, as well as whether it is unlined, lined, or even interlined.

The lightest weight is sheers, of transparent or translucent fabric. When deeply gathered, sheers filter light and offer privacy at the same time. Sheers are usually white or ecru but also come in colors. Extra-fine weaves of handkerchief-weight linen or organdy will produce a crisp sheer. Cotton batiste or lawn has the weight of a natural fiber but so fine a weave it creates a billowy translucent sheer that filters light with exquisite softness. Hung with triple fullness, its multiple layers are opaque enough to conceal a view or afford privacy without reducing the amount of light coming in.

Other soft, thin fabrics will also work as sheers, as well as any open-weave fabric such as gauze or net. Silk has a wonderful fluttery quality to the way it billows into folds. Just be sure to use it on a window that does not get direct sun. Translucent weaves of silk such as crepe, organza, finely pleated plisse, and georgette all make glorious sheers. However, treating several windows with maximum fullness requires many yards of fabric, so an economical approach to sheers is to use a synthetic fabric.

Curtains are in the light- to medium-weight range and are opaque. Lining them is optional, although it may be necessary for protection from the elements. Medium-weight cotton in the dress-weight range, especially very soft weaves like sea island and Egyptian cottons, floats voluptuously at a window and yet is substantial enough to fall in folds when puddled. Sheeting, chintz, poplin, and linen are all ideal candidates for curtain fabric.

Unbleached muslin is an excellent choice for curtain fabric; it is economical, 100 percent cotton, and because it is a natural fabric, it filters light beautifully and slowly bleaches to white in a few seasons. Its selvages may even feature a short, decorative edge.

Muslin comes in varying weights, each of which will produce a different quality of fold. Gauze is filmy enough to be used as a sheer. Medium-weight is semiopaque and produces a loose and

This simple runner valance, one-fifth the height of the window, is sewn with a slender casing with a crown. Instead of competing with a spectacular bay window view, this treatment invites one to sit and enjoy it. When making a casing with a crown, the crisper the fabric, like this fine linen, the better. Tight shirring contributes to the stiffened effect.

graceful fold. Heavyweight muslin approaches canvas in heft and creates a rich and uncommonly elegant effect for a fabric so ordinary and inexpensive.

Burlap is another economical fabric that filters light wonderfully and works well in a rustic or tai-

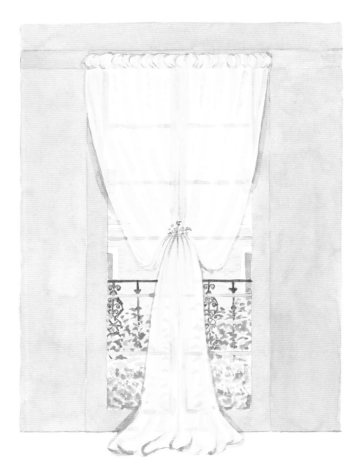

This single length of sheer silk plisse spills from a tieback holder fastened to the center frame of a French door and is puddled on the floor. This door, rarely opened, overlooks a balcony on a city street. At a frequently used French door two panels can be placed, one on each door. Sheers hung with extra full-

ness offer privacy without sacrificing light. Instead of sewing a casing, simply tape the fabric to a thin rod and roll it a few times to cover the tape. Any transparent fabric pliable enough to fall in soft folds can be used. Inexpensive sheer fabrics include muslin gauze, mosquito netting, and theatrical gauze.

lored setting. In its natural state, burlap is an ideal complement to many decorating schemes. Burlap is also available in colors.

Lace is a great favorite for curtain fabric. Dress-weight lace yardage usually has a small overall pattern and no border, unlike the slightly stiffer curtain-lace yardage, which is likely to have pattern motifs and a finished border with a design feature. Lace curtain yardage is less pliable than dress-weight lace but it has more substance. Lingerie lace can also be used for an ultra-feminine look.

Drapery panels that fall to the floor require the heaviest weight fabric. Consider any fabric from inexpensive cotton duck to luxurious fabrics like heavy chintz, damask, or brocade, as well as anything called drapery-weight fabric. For a sumptuous approach, choose velvet, chenille, tapestry, or heavy taffeta. Most upholstery-weight fabric is too stiff for drapery, but there are some exceptions. Such fabric may be suitable for a treatment consisting of one long length of fabric draped over swag holders and puddled slightly on the floor.

lining

Considerations of color apply especially to linings. Choose a sunny yellow or a warm rose as a contrasting lining to a panel, and it will enhance the panel's light-filtering qualities. Remember, however, that any color will fade if the window gets a lot of direct sun. Inexpensive muslin or a synthetic lining may then be the better choice.

It is sometimes necessary to use interlining as well as lining, especially if the color of a contrasting lining shows through to the panel. Interlining also provides extra protection for expensive drapery fabric and adds fullness to the folds of the treatment. Because it doesn't show, the interlining can be an old flannel sheet, a blanket, or even a quilt, depending upon how heavy you want the panel to be. It is also possible to create the luxurious look of heavy-weight fabric by interlining a beautiful medium-weight cotton; the window treatment not only looks elegant, it also becomes a barrier to the elements.

fabric width

The rule for the width of fabric for a window treatment is simple: the wider the better, especially for sheers, which come in widths from 60" to 72". Sometimes a bargain can be found in the narrower widths of 36" to 48", but if the panel is to be of double or triple fullness, you may need to piece it to achieve the necessary width, increasing the yardage requirements enormously. Also, with sheers the seams of a pieced panel are clearly visible.

Nevertheless, if you have your heart set on a narrower fabric or have found yourself a true bargain, instructions for piecing panels so that the seams are minimally visible are given in Sewing an Unlined Panel on page 87.

bed and table linens

Sheets are no longer the great bargain they once were, but they do have a terrific advantage when used in window treatments because of their extra width. Two twin sheets make an ideal pair of panels, with no sewing required at all. Extra-long sheets are a good choice for floor-length panels at tall windows. Even more generous are the dimensions of bedspreads, often with the bonus of many yards of fringe or other trim sewn around three sides. Bedskirts can be used as valances. Solid-color

bed linens or those with a nondirectional pattern are the most versatile for sewing panels because they can be cut in either direction.

The standard length of a twin- or full-size bedsheet is 96", and a queen- or king-size sheet is 102". When a rod is threaded through the facing on the top edge of a flat bedsheet, the sheet will most likely drop to the floor with extra inches that can be puddled. For tall windows, use a king-size sheet and hang it by its 108" width.

One queen-size sheet cut in half lengthwise will yield two panels of double fullness on a rod up to 43" in length. One king-size sheet cut the same way will cover a rod up to 51" in length. Left in one piece and drawn to one side, these large sheets will create a seamless window treatment.

Standard quilt sizes approximate those of bedsheets. Bedspreads makes jumbo-size window treatments. A twin-size bedspread is 80" by 110", queen-size is 102" by 120", and king-size is 120" square.

Tablecloths and linen towels can be used to create beautiful no-sew window treatments. Their dimensions should exceed that of the window, even if only slightly, to avoid a tight and skimpy look. Oval and round tablecloths and long lace runners, especially those with an interesting scalloped border, make beautiful valances or swags.

Sometimes the only thing to do with an oddly placed window is to ignore it, in this case behind a curtain of embroidered organza. The fabric is attached by clip-on rings to a thin strand of picture-frame wire supported by cup hooks every few feet to keep the wire from sagging. Dotted swiss, cutwork, and bedsheets are also good fabric choices for an entire wall.

What could be more extravagant than a heavy velvet drape in a deep, lush color? Here the fabric is doubly full and puddled to create extra richness. The flow of graceful curves is created by the diagonal tieback of cable cord attached over the rod. An economical approach to this elegant style is to use a fabric with nap, like brushed denim, no-wale corduroy, or other inexpensive plush in a deep color, and to line and interline it to create a look of heaviness to the folds. Large ornate tassels are often very expensive, but you can make one from a few inches of luxury drapery fringe.

vintage fabric

Because window treatments are exposed to the elements, it is rare to find vintage sheers or lightweight curtains. They simply do not hold up. Even heavy lined panels are often damaged where they are tied back, particularly when they have been pierced by a metal tieback holder. Nevertheless, the hues of natural fibers always improve with age. Even faded vintage panels can have a lot of character. Often they need to be lengthened or shortened. Consult the illustrations and the sewing instructions for ways to use vintage panels that are either damaged, too long, or too short without affecting the design features or cutting into the fabric unnecessarily.

trim and other embellishments

Giving a panel a border on all four sides not only looks beautiful, it conceals the finishing stitches on the edges of translucent fabric. Bands of ribbon or strips of organdy cut from yardage can be used. Silk ribbon looks especially attractive framing cotton, linen, or silk panels. Be careful using synthetic trims next to natural fabric; by contrast the synthetic color may look too bright and glaring.

Dressmaking and drapery fabric stores stock ribbons, edging, cord, fringe, and tassels in an enormous assortment of colors and designs. Dressmaking trim may seem too flimsy, but if it is applied in a double row it can look very luxurious, and it is much more economical than the heavier and more expensive drapery trim. The number of yards needed for trim around panels can add up surprisingly fast, and the cost of a pair of large decorative tassels for tiebacks can exceed that of the total yardage for the panel. However, it is possible to make tassels out of less than a yard of expensive fringe for a fraction of the cost of a ready-made tassel. See Sewing Tiebacks, on page 106.

Antique trims are also an option. Good drapery trim of silk, wool, or cotton ages particularly well and often outlasts the fabric it was intended to decorate. Keep an eye out for trim still attached to an otherwise unusable piece of cloth.

where to find fabric

Aside from a large department store, fabric for window treatments can be found in any retail outlet catering to the home sewer. It can also be ordered from swatches at paint and wallpaper stores, and at some home furnishing stores. Businesses that deal in slipcovering and upholstery and most interior decorators offer fabrics as well, but they may not be willing to do so independently of their sewing services.

bargains

Cut-rate quality fabrics can often be found at mill-end fabric stores, where "seconds" and surplus bolts of fabric are sold in job lots. Another good source is bargain stores that sell irregular bed linens. Look carefully because bargain stores offer good deals, but also lots of junk.

If you don't really know your fabric, bring along someone who does, or buy a yard and experiment with it. Do not purchase fabric off a bolt that is almost empty, because the next bolt may not have gone through the same dye lot. Make sure you examine every inch of the yardage on both sides to catch any irregularities in the weave, color, or printing.

Finally, don't overlook antiques stores, flea markets, yard and estate sales, and secondhand shops. Here you might find vintage panels, bed linens, tablecloths, and even old fabric still on the bolt. These can be the best discoveries of all.

before you buy

In the following chapter you will be given all the information needed to measure windows, calculate yardage, and prepare the fabric for draping or sewing. If you have a particular project in mind, check the sewing section first for any special requirements.

Now that you have a clear idea of what to look for in window treatment fabric, you will find when you make your shopping trip that many of the bewildering choices will already be eliminated, leaving just a few decisions. When you set out, know what you are looking for and how much you need ~ to the very inch, if buying luxury fabrics. And of course, always leave room for the unexpected find, particularly if it's a bargain.

ball fringe

CHAPTER THREE

getting started

The key to a simple and successful window treatment lies in good preparation. Before you begin, gather everything necessary for the project. Near the window, set up a clutter-free work space where you have enough room to cut, iron, and sew. And be sure to follow all the recommended preparations. All that steam pressing may seem tedious, but it will make a world of difference in the ease of sewing and finishing the edges of the panels and in the look of the finished window treatment. Once the fabric is cut, prepared, and ironed, the rest is easy.

window and hardware

A drapery rod
B finial
C drapery bracket
D soffit
E rod and bracket
  for sheers
F mullion
G sash
H tieback holder
I sill
J apron
K plinth
L frame

window treatment

M valance
N swag
O pouf
P tail
Q bishop sleeve
R tieback
S sheer
T panel
U Grecian folds
  (puddling)

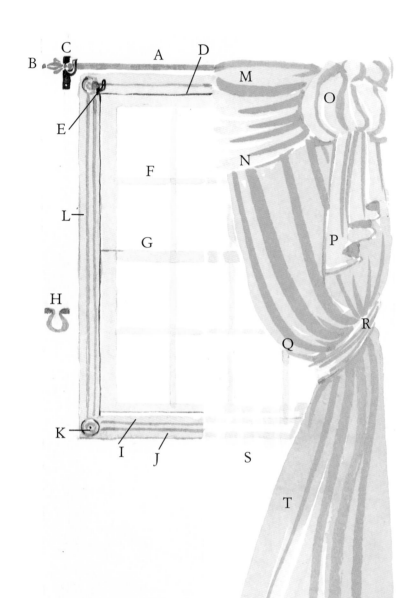

anatomy of a window treatment

Measuring a window involves familiarity with words unique to windows and window treatments. Using them as you measure will help eliminate confusion in an area where terms are far from standardized. The terms appear in the illustrations and in the specific instructions for measuring.

checklist

sewing materials

- [ ] Fabric
- [ ] Lining
- [ ] Interlining
- [ ] Trim
- [ ] Welting cord
- [ ] Thread
- [ ] Cloth tape measure
- [ ] Dressmaker's pins and pin cushion
- [ ] Silk pins
- [ ] Sewing needles: all purpose sharps, tapestry needle
- [ ] Sewing machine needles: #9 (65) for extra light-weight; #11–14 (75–90) for light to medium weight; #16–18 (100–110) for heavier-weight fabric
- [ ] Sewing machine zipper foot
- [ ] Velcro
- [ ] Shirring tape (mesh for sheers)
- [ ] Medium-size safety pin or loop-and-tubing turner
- [ ] Drapery tape
- [ ] White or ecru embroidery thread
- [ ] ½"-wide iron-on fusing tape
- [ ] Sewing shears: 5" blades or longer
- [ ] Small, sharp-tipped scissors for clipping

household items

- [ ] Steam iron and ironing board
- [ ] Pocket calculator
- [ ] Pressing cloth
- [ ] Spray mister
- [ ] Yardstick
- [ ] T-square
- [ ] #2 pencil
- [ ] 2"-wide masking tape
- [ ] Pushpins
- [ ] Butcher's twine (medium-weight twisted cord)
- [ ] Stepladder or stool

hardware

- [ ] Staple gun and staples
- [ ] Glue gun
- [ ] Hammer and 1" headless nails
- [ ] Screwdriver and small screws
- [ ] Picture-frame wire, single strand
- [ ] Large-size cup hooks used for hanging mugs
- [ ] Swag or tieback holders
- [ ] Rod or dowel and brackets
- [ ] 1x3 or 1x4 lumber cut to size for mounting board
- [ ] Electric drill

sewing supplies

Whether your window treatment requires sewing or not, you will need a good pair of shears and a yardstick for measuring. Check the requirements for individual projects and make sure you have whatever items are necessary before you begin. The checklist of supplies at left is designed to help you take inventory. Most items can be found at hardware or lumber stores, the drapery section of a department store, a fabric store, or a dime store.

establishing a work space

A window treatment often requires multiple yards of fabric that need to be measured and cut on a table or the floor. A kitchen or dining table with a pad makes an excellent work surface. Set up the ironing board close to your work space, as you will be steam pressing seams frequently throughout the sewing process. Wherever you work, be sure to clean the floor before you begin to protect any fabric that spills onto the floor as you are cut, drape, iron, and sew.

preparing the window

Remove any existing window treatment and clean the window thoroughly. If hardware has not been installed, follow the instructions in Attachments, page 122, for placement and installation of rods, brackets, swag and tieback holders, and mounting boards.

measuring the window

Two measurements need to be taken, and they are unique to window treatments: Length is called the drop and is measured from the top of the rod downward to the desired edge of the hem. The width of the window treatment is called the length of the rod.

To measure the window, you will need a stepladder or stool, a pad and pencil, and a yardstick. Measure the width and length of the window treatment. Based on these two measurements, you can determine how much yardage you need.

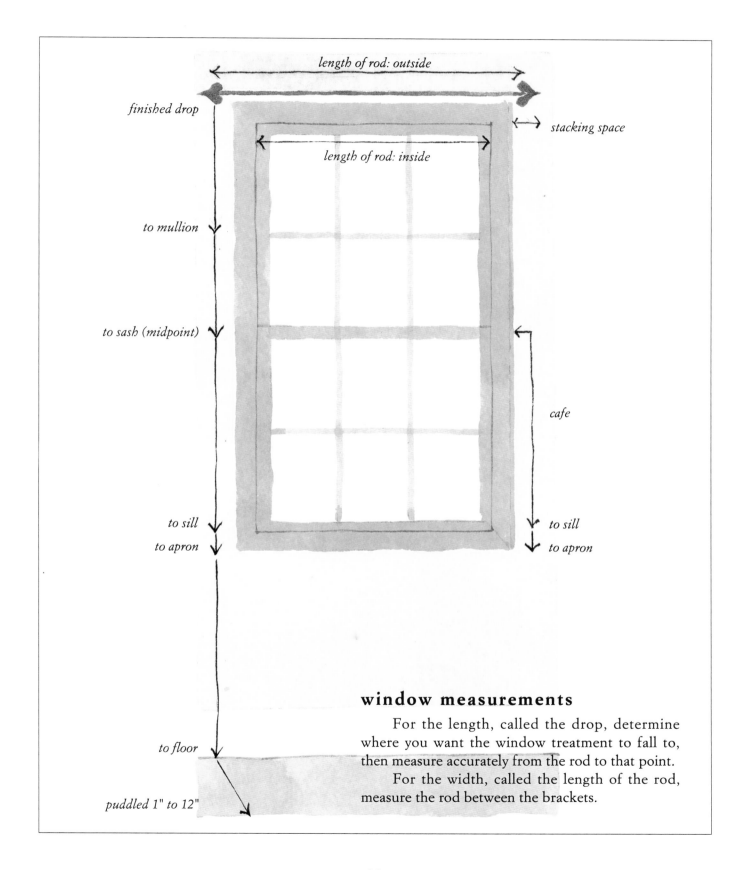

length of rod: outside

finished drop

stacking space

length of rod: inside

to mullion

to sash (midpoint)

cafe

to sill

to apron

to sill

to apron

to floor

window measurements

For the length, called the drop, determine where you want the window treatment to fall to, then measure accurately from the rod to that point.

For the width, called the length of the rod, measure the rod between the brackets.

puddled 1" to 12"

measuring the finished drop

The drop is measured from the top of the rod to the following:

From rod to bottom of valance. When used with panels, valances are traditionally one-fifth of the drop of the panel. The drop can also fall to the first horizontal line of a mullion, or as far as needed to conceal the wall above the window, if the rod is extended above the window frame. If the valance you are going to make has a curved or diagonal bottom edge, measure the drop to the lowest point.

From rod to sill. Panels hung inside a window frame usually look best dropping to the sill. This level is also used for a panel that is a bit too short to use otherwise.

From rod to apron. Panels hung outside a window look best when they extend to the bottom of the window frame.

From rod to floor. Long panels look best when they drop all the way to the floor rather than an inch or two above it, which can produce a "highwater" look that does not enhance the way the fabric falls.

From rod to floor, puddled. An additional 1" to 12" beyond the drop to the floor will produce panels that fall in Grecian folds. One inch will loosen the vertical line of the folds without really puddling. Two inches are recommended for panels with a border, such as a welted hem, ribbon band, or lace edging, to allow the design feature to show at the bottom edge. Six to twelve inches extra produce a generous puddled effect.

From the rod to wherever you please. There are no hard-and-fast rules concerning where a panel should fall. The bottom edge can also be measured at any point between the apron and the floor that you desire, especially if it is dictated by a design in the panel, wainscotting, or your furnishings.

Cafe. Measure cafe curtains from sash or midpoint of a casement window to the sill if you are hanging the curtain inside the window. Measure it from sash or midpoint to the apron for an outside window treatment. However, cafes do not necessarily have to begin at the sash level. If you want to create more privacy, accommodate a fabric with a border or other distinctive feature, or are treating a small or sashless window, the cafe rod can be placed wherever you like.

measuring the unfinished drop

The measurements of the following features must be added to the finished drop. (Check individual sewing projects for specific requirements.)

Self-valance. The fabric of a self-valance is not cut separately but is an extension of the panel that is folded over the rod and given a casing. See Measuring the Finished Drop of the valance, above, to determine the number of inches required, and add 1" for a hem.

Faced heading. Add ½".

Casing and crown. See individual projects in Casings (page 91) to determine the amount needed.

Bishop sleeve. Add 3" to 12" depending on the depth of the curve you want to create at the tieback.

Hem. Add ½" for sheers with a handkerchief hem, 2" for lightweight curtains, and 4" for heavyweight panels with a double turned hem.

Repeats. Measure the lengthwise distance between the repeats (see Repeat, page 137). Double that number and multiply it by the number of yards in the finished drop. For example, if the finished drop is 2 yards and the repeat is 6", add 24". For large-pattern motifs, begin or end the measurement with a complete motif, so that it creates a border at the heading or at the hem.

Add any additions above to the measurement of the finished drop to get the total length of the unfinished drop.

measuring the length of the rod

When attaching brackets for the rod, allow space between the brackets and the edge of the window, called the stacking space, where the panels will sit when they are pulled back so they will clear the window and not cut down on the amount of light that enters the room. For lightweight fabrics or moderately full panels, attaching the brackets 3" to 4" beyond the frame leaves adequate stacking space. Heavyweight fabric and extra-full panels need a stacking space of from 6" to 12" if they are going to clear the window when open. To determine the width of the window treatment, measure the length of the rod from bracket to bracket.

If the treatment requires no rod, measure the distance from the left to right edge of the window or mounting board. For an inside window treatment, measure the width of the inside frame of the window.

determining the width of the heading

To determine the unfinished width of the heading, the top edge of a panel, divide the length of the rod by the number of panels you are making and add 2" for side seam allowances for each panel.

Decide how full you want the panels to be. If only slight fullness is desired, one and a half times the width of the heading is recommended, for medium- to heavyweight fabric, double fullness, and for sheers, triple fullness.

calculating the yardage

The following is a formula for determining the yardage needed for a single panel.

1. Determine the width of the heading: divide the length of the rod by the number of panels and add 2" for seams.

2. Multiply the sum determined in Step 1 by the desired fullness described above.

3. Divide the width of the fabric from selvage to selvage by the sum of Step 2. If the quotient has a remainder, go for extra fullness whenever possible and use a full width of fabric.

For example:
The length of the rod is 40" and a pair of panels is needed. The fabric is 60" wide, and double

fullness is desired.
Step 1. 40" divided by 2 = 20", plus 2 = 22"
Step 2. 22" x 2 = 44"
Step 3. 60" divided by 44" = 1.36, rounded off to 1
Result: One panel requires a single width of fabric, with an extra 16" for additional fullness, or piecing if it is necessary to scrimp.

4. Multiply the sum of Step 3 (in this case 1) by the number of inches in the unfinished drop and divide by 36" to determine the yardage needed for a single panel. When sewing more than one panel, multiply that number by the number of panels to determine total yardage required.

piecing

When the quotient in Step 3 of the formula to determine yardage is less than one, it will be necessary to piece in order to achieve the desired fullness (see Piecing, page 87). One extra length of fabric can be cut in half lengthwise and used as part of the yardage for a pair of panels.

measuring a swag

Swags are simply panels hung across the window. They can be pieced at the points where they are tied back or caught up in a swag holder, where the seams won't show. If the swag has a diagonal bottom, measure to the deepest point.

1. Measure the drop from the rod to the bottom edge of the swag and multiply by two. (If the bottom edges are not the same length, measure each drop separately and add them together.)

2. Measure the length of the rod.

3. If the swag is to drop in the center of the window, exposing the rod, measure the drop at the center of the window from the rod to the top of the swag. Add the results of Steps 1, 2, and 3.

how to scrimp

- Use a solid or nondirectional fabric without a nap.

- Use fabric that is 60" or wider.

- Railroad the valance (see page 137).

- Piece the panels.

- Use slight to moderate fullness and add lining for extra body.

- Use a hem with contrasting welting.

- Drop the rod a few inches and treat the top of the window with a valance.

- Hang a curtain inside the window, dropped to the sill.

- Piece a valance or swag and conceal the seams behind a swag holder at the corners or center of the window.

- Use two complementary fabrics in one panel or on the same rod.

- Add a decorative border.

- Sew on fringe or trim.

- Use longer tabs.

- Use a panel that is too short as a deep swag or valance.

preparing the fabric

Fabric for a window treatment does not have to be elaborately prepared. All it usually needs is a thorough steam pressing and it is ready to be draped or sewn.

preshrinking

Shrinkage is not necessarily bad, for it makes a fabric weave tighter and stronger. But you don't want it to occur after you have made the window treatment, and have the length of the panels become shorter or the seams wrinkle because the lining has shrunk and the fabric has not. Consequently, preshrinking is recommended for lined panels.

Nevertheless, try to avoid preshrinking most fabric, especially unlined panels, for the fabric is much easier to work with straight from the bolt. Sizing, a starchlike substance used to treat most bedsheets, cotton, and cotton blends during manufacturing, gives it crispness that adds body. Rather than preshrinking the fabric, add an extra inch or two to the drop and fold it up into the hem for lengthening later if needed.

dry cleaning

Plan to dry-clean lined panels that have not been preshrunk. Check any information on selvages regarding cleaning instructions. Sometimes the words "Dry Clean Only" are clearly printed there. Other fabric may not be marked with cleaning instructions, but if it is silk, or has a nap or a treated surface, such as on chintz or damask, it should be dry-cleaned. Make note of cleaning instructions for the future, as you may cut off the selvages when you prepare the fabric.

color fastness

If you want to be able to wash the panels, test the fabric as follows: Wash a strip of fabric, lining, and any cloth trim separately in a bowl of soapy water to determine whether the colors are fast. If color bleeds into the wash water, you will need to dry-clean the panel.

laundering gauze

Gauze often contains a lot of sizing which gives it more body on the bolt. This is particularly true of bargain cotton gauzes like muslin. If the fabric feels crisp, launder in very hot water and dry it in a hot dryer. Before steam pressing, pull the selvages on the diagonal in both directions along the length of the cloth to further loosen up the weave.

the wrinkled look

Muslin can look wonderful left in an unironed state, particularly when draped in Grecian folds.

Launder as for gauze, and take the fabric out of the dryer while still damp. Hang it from a clothes line or shower rod. When it dries, it will be nicely crinkled.

steam pressing

With the exception of muslin gauze that has been deliberately wrinkled, all window treatments look best when given a thorough steam pressing in the preparation process. Steam pressing compresses the fibers on the surface to create a polished sheen that also helps shed dust. Pre-dampen linen and cotton and set the iron to the hottest setting. Linen fibers are especially stiff and the fabric needs to be dampened and tightly rolled in plastic for a few hours before ironing.

Steam press silk and synthetics using a damp linen pressing cloth with the iron set on cotton. When working with chintz or other fabrics with a sheen or a raised surface, always steam press on the wrong side. Iron lace with a damp pressing cloth and the iron set to linen. Be especially careful with handworked lace such as crochet, arranging it on the ironing board a few inches at a time to keep the longer threads of the design smoothly in place.

straightening the grain

Fabric is not always folded straight on the bolt, and the crosswise edge may not have been cut evenly when it was cut from the bolt. Before steam pressing, fold the fabric right side in so the selvage edges meet between your fingers. Collect folds of selvages between your fingers and give the fabric a good shake. Working a yard at a time pin the selvages together, shaking the fold and smoothing the surface until the fold lies flat. Steam press the fold as you iron the length of the fabric; it will become a lengthwise grid line, useful when you cut or piece panels.

evening the edges

The cutting edge of the fabric must be trimmed perpendicular to the selvage edges because it will determine all future cutting lines. Square off the crosswise edge using a T square, or line the sel-vage edge along one side of a table near the corner and square off using the edge of the table as a guide.

selvage edges

Leave the selvage edges of no-sew window treatments intact as they keep the sides from raveling; steam press them under, turning ½" to the wrong side. Cut off the selvages of panels that will be sewn, because their woven edge can be seen through the hemlines of sheers and they do not lie flat when seamed or folded under.

preparing the edges for finishing

After you have cut the pieces of panel and lining, steam press the folding creases on all four sides and corners of the fabric and lining. Consult individual project instructions for information on how much fabric will be turned under. Also steam press under the ¼" folds of a handkerchief hem before you begin sewing. Most edges should be folded under, steam pressed flat, and folded under again. When you sew, the fabric will then fold in place neatly for stitching, or the creases will be a guide for where seam lines begin, end, and are reinforced.

steam mitering corners

Follow the instructions for the mitered corner on page 136. Rather than pinning or stitching, steam press a crease in the folds created in the mitering process, especially the diagonal fold, which is difficult to fold under in a straight line with fingers alone. Steam press it carefully so its edges abut and meet the folds above and below the diagonal. Be particularly careful steam pressing mitered corners on sheers and lightweight unlined panels.

Your fabric is now ready to be sewn.

CHAPTER FOUR

sewing a window treatment

Sewing a window treatment is a simple task because, unlike dressmaking or slipcovering, it involves only two dimensions ~ length and width ~ eliminating the need for fitting around curves. Depth, the third dimension, is created naturally when fabric is folded, pleated, or gathered onto a rod. Only turning the corners requires any real skill, and the technique of mitering is greatly simplified by using a steam iron.

The instructions in this chapter cover sewing unlined and lined panels, valances, swags, and tiebacks. In the directions, the heading is the top of a panel, where fullness is created and the casing or attachments are sewn. The sides are the vertical edges of the panels, and hems are the bottom edge.

sewing an unlined panel

Before you begin, prepare the fabric for cutting, following the instructions in Getting Started, page 84. Cut each panel needed to the unfinished length and width as instructed on page 82.

matching patterns

To calculate the extra yardage a repeated pattern may require, see Measuring the Unfinished Drop, page 82. When working with fabric that has a pattern, make sure that the repeat is uniformly matched on each section. Use the first panel as a guide for cutting additional panels or sections of a panel by positioning the first panel over the fabric to be cut so that the motif matches at the top and bottom edges (Figure 1). To match pattern motifs along a seam, pin right sides together, folding back the upper edge every few inches to make sure specific details of the pattern are matching.

piecing

If the fabric is narrower than the required width of a panel, you will need to piece it. Always sew the narrower piece to the edge of the wider sec-tion on the side that will hang closer to the wall, where it will be less obvious, not the center edge.

Cut a second panel the same length as the first and as wide as needed to complete the required dimensions, plus ½" for a seam allowance. For example, if you need width 72" and the fabric is 48" wide, cut the second piece 24½" wide (Figure 2). With right sides together, pin the long edges of the panels. Stitch ½" from the edge and steam press the seam allowance open. Finish sheers with a flat-felled seam (page 134).

sewing the heading

The heading is the top of a panel, where extra fullness can be made by pleating or gathering the fabric using the following methods.

box pleat

1. Along the side edges, fold under ½" and steam press. Fold under ½" again and steam press.

2. Place the panel wrong side up and, starting at the edge of the heading that will be in the

FIGURE 1
matching patterns

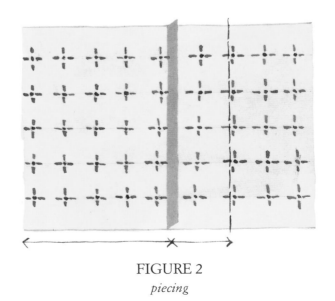

FIGURE 2
piecing

center of the window, make a pencil mark at 4" intervals across the raw edge. If the last marking is more or less than 4" do not be concerned. The pleat will be adjusted later. Label the first five pencil marks A, B, C, B, A. Then label each subsequent group of five marks the same way. The last sequence may be incomplete; this will be adjusted later.

3. With the panel right side up, make each box pleat by bringing the A marks together and folding on the B marks (Figure 1). Pin to secure. If the last pleat is wider or narrower than the others, repin the last two pleats to adjust the folds at the A mark to compensate for too much or too little fabric in the final pleat.

4. Steam press the pleats along the top two inches of the heading, then stitch the pleats ½" from the edge, stitching on the right side of the fabric. If you are using tabs, see Sewing Tabs, page 95, before proceeding.

5. To finish the raw edges of the heading, cut a strip of facing from the fabric or a piece of muslin that is 2" wide and as long as the heading plus 2". Steam press under a ½" fold along one of its long edges and the two sides. Steam press an additional ½" fold on the two sides. With right sides together, pin the facing to the heading, matching raw edges, and stitch along the top of the heading ½" in from the edge, reinforcing at both ends.

6. Trim the seam and fold the facing over to the back of panel. Steam press the folded edge flat. Slip stitch the folded sides of the facing to the panel.

7. Secure the bottom edge of the facing with a slip stitch, catching the underlayers of the pleat so that the front of the panel is seamless.

machine-shirred heading

This heading can be taped or stapled to a mounting board for a stationary panel (or valance) or it can be given a casing and hung on a rod if you want the curtain to open and close. For each panel you will need a length of shirring tape equal to the unfinished width of the panel.

1. On the side edges, turn under ½" and steam press. Turn under ½" again and steam press.

2. To face the top raw edge and make a casing, measure the diameter of the rod and add ½" for a seam allowance and an additional ½" for easing on and off the rod. Fold the raw edge ½" to the wrong side and steam press. Measure down from the fold the number of inches needed for the casing, fold the fabric, and steam press the fold. Do not sew the casing, as it will be sewn when the first line of shirring stitches is made.

3. Lay the heading wrong side up and

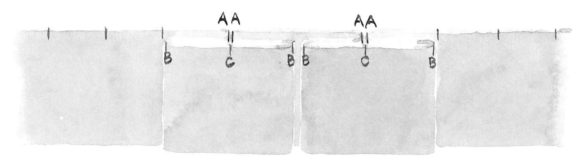

FIGURE 1
box pleats

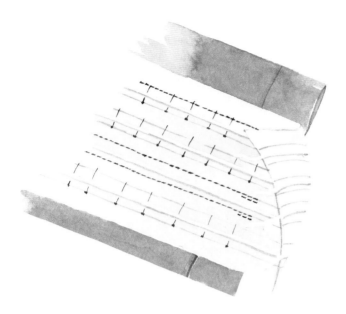

FIGURE 2
machine shirring

place the shirring tape over it, right side up, with the top stitching line overlapping the fold of the heading by ½" (Figure 2). Pin along the top cord, putting the pins perpendicular to the top edge.

4. Leaving the first and last inch free for finishing, slowly stitch a line above the cord, directly over the stitching line marked on the tape, reinforcing at both ends. In the process you will also be sewing the seam line of the casing. In the same way stitch a line below the cord, directly over the stitching lines marked on the tape, removing the pins as you go. Stitch slowly and accurately so you don't stitch into the cord itself.

5. Repeat Step 4 for all the cords, making sure to leave the first and last inches free for finishing. At one side, stitch across the rows 1" in from the edge to secure the ends of the cords for pulling; leave the opposite end of the cords free.

6. At the free end, gently pull each cord until the shirring is the desired fullness. To secure, wind the tail of each cord around a pin, then stitch across the rows at the fold. Trim off the excess cord and tape to ½". Fold under the raw edges of the shirring tape and slip stitch to the fold. Slip stitch the folds along the side edges.

7. If you are shirring both the top and bottom of a panel, stitch the shirring tape to the bottom edge exactly as you did for the top.

hand-shirred heading

Lace looks best with hand-stitched rows of shirring because the many stitching lines of machine shirring may show in the openwork of the pattern, while hand-stitched shirring all but disappears into the folds of gathering. For the gathering stitches, you will need six-strand embroidery thread and a blunt-tipped tapestry needle.

1. To make a casing, follow Step 2 for the machine-shirred heading on page 88.

2. Cut a piece of embroidery thread that is as long as the heading and separate it into two 3-strand pieces. Using one of the triple strands, insert the needle ¼" below the casing seam line (Figure 1), reinforce with several stitches, then bring the tapestry needle through the lace to form several running stitches. Continue to sew tiny running stitches, in a straight line along the casing seam line. At the end of the row, draw the thread through and leave it uncut.

3. Repeat Step 2 to make a second row of running stitches ¼" below the first row. Depending on how deep you want the shirring, make two to six additional rows in the same manner.

4. Take the loose ends of the embroidery thread between two fingers and gently pull to gather, adjusting the fullness as you pull the threads until the panel is the desired width. Stitch to reinforce the pulling ends of the thread and cut off the excess thread.

5. If the sides of the lace have raw edges, hem them following the instructions for a handkerchief hem, page 100.

sewing a facing to a heading

A heading without a casing, such as a panel that will be attached with rings, needs to be finished with a facing.

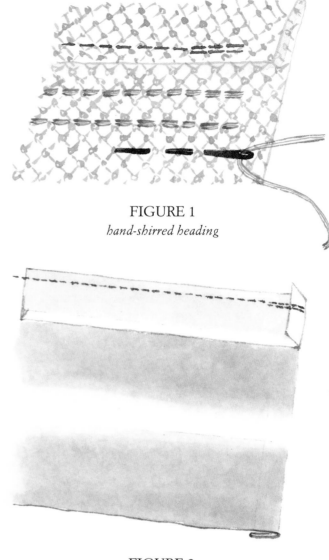

FIGURE 1
hand-shirred heading

FIGURE 2
faced heading

1. Cut a strip of fabric, preferably the same fabric as the panel, 2" wide and as long as the unfinished heading. Steam press under a ½" fold along one of its long edges and the two sides. Steam press another ½" fold on the two sides.

2. With right sides together, pin the raw edge of the facing to the heading and stitch a seam ½" from the edge, reinforcing at both ends (Figure 2).

3. Clip the seam allowances and steam press the seam open. Fold the facing to the wrong side of the panel and steam press flat.

4. Blind stitch or fuse the bottom edge of the facing to the wrong side of the panel. Slip stitch the folded sides of the facing to the panel.

casings

Casings fulfill two needs: to attach the panel to the rod and to gather fullness in a heading. Gathering can be achieved without shirring by making a snugly fitting casing that will gather the fabric into folds that range in fullness from slightly gathered, using less than double the panel width, to full ruching, three times the panel width. There are several different ways to make a casing.

self-casing

A self-casing is made by folding the top of the panel over and stitching a seam, creating a channel for the rod to go through. As this simple casing lacks a decorative finish, it can be used for headings that will be covered by a valance or for fine fabrics such as sheers and lace, for which a minimal casing contributes to the light and airy nature of the curtain.

1. Fold under the sides of the panel ½" to the wrong side and steam press. Fold under ½" again and steam press. The side edges will be finished later.

2. To determine the width of the casing, encircle the rod with a tape measure to find the circumference and divide that number in half. Add 1" for seam allowances. For ease of movement add an

self-casing

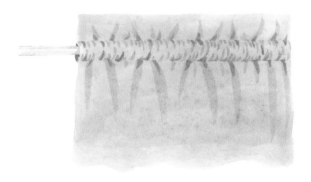

casing with a crown

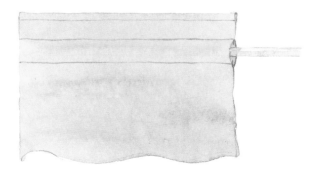

rod pocket casing

ruched casing with matching covered rod

extra ½" for lightweight and 1" for medium- to heavyweight fabrics. This allowance will help in getting the panel on and off the rod and will reduce stress on the casing.

3. With the fabric wrong side up, fold the top edge of the heading back the required width determined in Step 2 and steam press. Fold the top edge back on itself a second time and steam press the new fold. If the panel is too short for a double casing, do not make the second fold. If you have enough fabric, do make the reinforced casing because it is where the most wear on the panel takes place.

4. Stitch the casing ¼" from the inside fold, reinforcing at both ends. (Figure 1).

FIGURE 1
sewing a self-casing

rod pocket casing

This casing is used when a panel has a design feature, such as a border or trim, that needs to be kept intact, or when scrimping. Instead of folding the top edge over, a strip of fabric or bias tape is sewn to the wrong side of the panel.

1. Fold the sides of the panel ½" to the wrong side and steam press. Fold under ½" again and steam press. The edges will be finished later.

2. To determine the width of the casing, follow Step 2 for the self-casing at the left.

3. If the rod pocket is narrow, use bias tape that has a ¼" folded hem. If the rod pocket is wider than 2", cut a strip of muslin or, for translucent fabric, a strip of fabric that blends with the fabric of the panel, to the dimensions determined in Step 2. Fold under the two long edges ¼" and steam press.

4. Pin the tape or strip of facing to the wrong side of the heading (Figure 2) and stitch next to the fold on both edges of the casing.

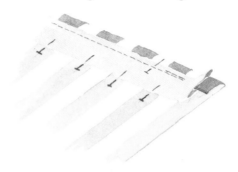

FIGURE 2
sewing a rod pocket casing

casing with crown

There are practical as well as aesthetic reasons for using a casing with a crown. It provides an elegant shirred border above the rod, and it screens out the sliver of bright sun at the top of a window with an eastern or southern exposure. A tightly gathered casing with a crown gives a finished look to a window treatment without a valance. Crowns higher than 2" need to be stiffened so that the heading stands upright.

1. Fold under the sides of the panel ½" to the wrong side and steam press. Fold under ½" again and steam press. The edges will be finished later.

2. Follow Step 2 for self-casing to determine the width of the casing.

3. Decide the height of the crown, from a minimal ½" for sheers to a maximum of 4" for heavyweight draperies. Multiply by two. Add the sum of Step 2 and Step 3.

4. To stiffen a high crown, iron a strip of medium-weight interfacing the height of the finished crown to the wrong side of the top edge of the fabric, ¼" down from the top edge.

5. Fold under ¼" along the top edge of the heading and steam press.

6. On the wrong side of the heading mark with a pin the measurement determined at the conclusion of Step 3. Bring the top edge down to meet the pin line. Repin, and stitch close to the folded edge (Figure 3), reinforcing at both ends.

7. Stitch the inner seam line of the casing at the width determined in Step 2, reinforcing it at both ends.

FIGURE 3
sewing a casing with crown

ruched casing with matching covered rod

This casing treats the top edge of a window treatment, the casing, and the rod, all in one. It is the ideal way to cap off a window without reducing the light or using a valance or cornice, and it is a way to complete the top when the drapery panels do not meet in the center of the rod. Panels need to be twice the width for medium- to heavyweight fabric and triple width for sheers in order to produce the tightly gathered folds characteristic of ruching. To cover the rod, a long strip of fabric is sewn and then gathered tightly as it is pulled onto the exposed section of the rod. It need not be sewn to the panels. The result is a single narrow line of gathering that creates a simple yet elegant crown to a window treatment.

1. On the side edges of the panel, fold ½" to the wrong side and steam press. Fold under ½" again and steam press. These edges will be finished later. To form a ruched casing, sew a self-casing, page 91, using maximum fullness.

2. To make a ruched covering for the rod, measure the circumference of the rod, add 1" for seams, and add an additional ½" for sheers and 1" for heavier fabric for easing. This is the width of the casing strip.

3. To determine the length of casing needed, measure the section of the rod left open between the panels and multiply by six for sheers, by four for medium-weight, and by three for heavyweight fabric. It may be necessary to cut more than one strip for the length. If so, sew the pieces end to end with ½" seams to make one long strip.

4. Adjust the stitch regulator to 18–20 stitches per inch. Fold the strip in half and match up the two raw edges. Stitch ½" from the edge, reinforcing well at the beginning and the end.

5. Using a loop-and-tubing turner or inserting a medium-size safety pin into the raw edge of one of the openings, turn the tube right side out (Figure 1).

FIGURE 1
turning the tube

6. Slip the tube onto the rod and gather. Even out the ruching so it is uniformly tight. It is not necessary to finish the ends because you can tuck the raw edges under.

casing with self-valance

Due to its construction, this casing works only with fabric that is the same on both sides. It is an ideal way to shorten an existing panel or give a finished look to the exposed heading of a panel.

1. Determine the finished drop of the valance, usually about one fifth the length of the panel. The valance size can also be determined by other factors such as a window mullion, a motif repeat, or the need to conceal the wall of an extended mounting board. Add an additional 1" for a hem.

2. To determine the width of the casing, follow the instructions in Step 2 for sewing a self-casing, page 92. Add that sum to the sum total of Step 1 above to determine the fold line.

3. Fold under ½" along the side edges and steam press. Fold under ½" again and steam press. At the top edge fold under the fabric to form the self-valance and steam press. Mark a line with pins the width of the casing determined in Step 2,

then stitch a seam line (Figure 2). At the side edges the fold will be on the right side of the valance; blind stitch the fold to the valance.

4. To hem the valance, fold the raw edge under ½" and steam press. Fold under ½" again and steam press. Attach trim or hem with a blind stitch or fusing tape. Do not use a machine-stitched hem because the line of stitching will be visible.

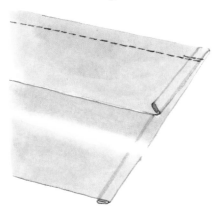

FIGURE 2
sewing a casing with a self-valance

tabs and ties

Tabs attach panels to a drapery rod. The two raw ends of a tab are sewn into the seam line of an unfinished heading, creating a loop through which a rod is inserted. Wide tabs are used to support heavyweight or multiple layers of fabric, especially lined box pleats. The wider the tab, the more secure the attachment. Narrow tabs create natural pleats when an unlined panel is drawn back from the window. And tabs can be made longer when there is a need to lengthen the panel.

Ties are a charming but nonfunctional decorative touch, as it is not necessary to untie them to remove the panel from the rod. Ties are made like tabs but folded in half with the fold sewn into the heading seam line, leaving the two ends free for tying in a knot or a bow. Tabs and ties can be made of the same fabric as the panel, or they can become a design feature, made of the contrasting lining, a

wide tabs

narrow tabs

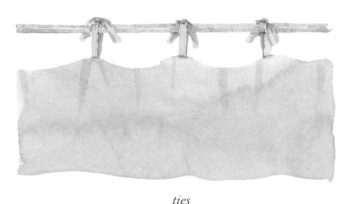

ties

tabs of decorative tape

striped or patterned fabric cut on the bias, or decorative ribbons, cord, or woven drapery tape, or other trim with finished edges that can be purchased by the yard.

sewing tabs

1. Determine the finished width of tab you want to use. The recommended maximum width is 2" and the minimum is ¼". Determine the length of the tab by encircling the rod with a cloth tape measure and allowing an extra 2" for easing and seams. Allow additional inches if you want to lengthen the panel.

2. If the finished width of the tab is to be ½" or wider, multiply by two and add 1" for seam allowances. Cut as many strips as you need to that width and the length determined in Step 1. You

will need a tab every 4" to 6" along the heading. If you are cutting bias strips, follow the instructions for cutting bias strips, page 131.

3. Fold the tab in half right sides together so the long edges meet. Stitch a seam ½" from the edge, and trim the seam.

sewing a tab

95

4. Steam press the seam open and turn the tab right side out. Steam press again. Sew the remaining tabs in the same manner.

5. If the width of the finished tab is to be narrower than ½", cut strips 1" wide and as long as determined in Step 1 above.

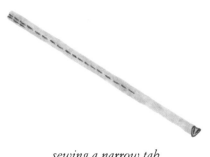

sewing a narrow tab

6. Steam press under ¼" along the long edges of the tie. Fold the tie so the folded edges meet and steam press again. Stitch a seam down the middle of the two folds.

7. On the wrong side of the unfinished heading, mark with a pencil the points where you want the tabs to be sewn, leaving 2" free at each end for finishing. If sewing a heading with box pleats, the tabs are placed where the two folds of each box pleat join in the middle. This holds the pleat in place when the panel is hung. Pin all tabs and sew them ½" from the edge, reinforcing several times over, especially the first and last tabs which will receive

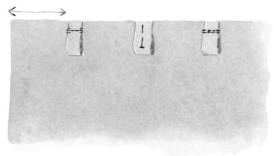

sewing tabs to the heading

the most tugging when the panel is opened and closed. To finish the heading, follow the instructions in Sewing a Facing to a Heading, for an unlined panel, page 90, or in Curtain Lining for Unfinished Heading, for a lined panel, page 102.

sewing ties

Ties are cut and sewn like tabs but attached in the middle, leaving the ends free. Follow Steps 1–6 for sewing tabs. If the ties are wider than ½", fold the raw edges of the ends under and slip stitch the folds together. Raw edges on ends of narrower ties can be left unsewn.

1. Mark with a pencil on the wrong side of the heading where the ties will be sewn, about every 4" to 6", leaving 2" free at each end for finishing. Fold a tie in half and pin the fold ¼" below the seam line. Pin the rest of the ties in the same manner. Stitch several times through each tie on the seam line, giving extra reinforcement to the first and last ties.

2. To finish the heading, follow the instructions for the heading with a facing for an unlined panel, page 90, or for unfinished headings for a lined panel, page 102.

rings

Rings are a simple and pleasing way to create fullness in a window treatment without gathering or pleating. Rings are sewn along the heading every 4" to 6"; when the panel is closed, deep folds form between the rings .

There are three ways to attach rings. The simplest is the clip-on ring. When the sides of the ring are pinched together the teeth open slightly, allowing it to grip the fabric when pressure is released. Clip-on rings will support sheers and lightweight fabric, but not heavyweight fabric, lined panels, or those with pleated headings.

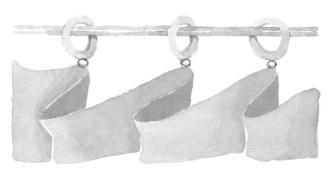

washable plastic rings

detachable wooden rings

washable rings

Sew white plastic and brass rings onto the wrong side of the heading, making stitches into the fabric and over the ring. The rings can be sewn several inches from the top of the heading or at the bottom edge of a band, creating a fold-over valance. Rings can be left on during washings.

detachable rings

Large wooden drapery rings have a small screw eye fastened to them through which the thread is stitched. When the panels have to be cleaned, the threads are snipped with small scissors; the rings are then stitched on again before the panels are hung back on the rod.

An alternative to sewing and resewing is to attach the ring with a paper clip. Sew the paper clip onto the wrong side of the heading, $\frac{1}{2}$" below the finished edge. Thread the eye of the ring through the free end of the paper clip; detach before cleaning.

Wooden rings can be painted, stained, varnished, or simply left in their natural state. They can be used with all weights of fabric and with lined panels; however, they are not recommended for attaching lined pleated draperies because the weight of the multiple folds may pull loose the tiny screw eye.

attaching a ring with a paper clip

clip-on rings

finishing the edges with bands

Bands can define all four edges of a window treatment to form an elegant frame-within-a-frame. They are practical as well as aesthetic because they conceal the seams, and the mitered corners help weight the edges so that very fine fabrics will hang more substantially.

self-band

The self-band forms a tailored flanged border on all four sides of a panel without a casing at the top, or around three sides of a panel with a casing. It is created by folding the edges and topstitching in from the fold, adding definition to the corners and weighting the edges. It also finishes both sides of the panel.

1. Determine the width of the band desired, usually from 1" to 2", then add ½" for finishing the edge.

2. Fold under ½" on all four sides of the panel and steam miter the corners following the instructions on page 136.

3. Fold under another 1" to 2" to form the band and steam miter the corners again as in Step 2. On the right side of the fabric, pin the corners to secure them while you topstitch.

4. Adjust the stitch regulator to 6–8 stitches per inch and topstitch 1" to 2" in from the edge of the panel, thus forming a band on all four sides. Stitch around the corners carefully, because you will be stitching through the extra layers of fabric of the mitered corners.

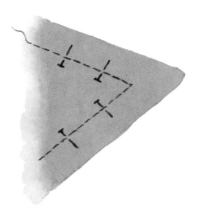

topstitching a self-band

bias band

A bias band of the same fabric makes an attractive frame for a panel of patterned fabric, particularly a plaid or stripe. It is especially suited to woven fabric, making the window treatment reversible inside and out.

1. Decide the width you would like the bias band to be ~ a finished width of 1" to 3" is recommended, depending on the scale of the window treatment and the fabric. A delicate striped lawn curtain would look best with a narrow band of 1" to 2", while a large plaid would look best with a 3" band. To the finished width of the band add 1" for seam allowances.

2. Measure the drop of the finished panel and measure the heading. Multiply the sum of those two numbers by two to determine the number of inches of bias strip you will need. Divide by 36" to determine the yardage. One-half yard of 48"-wide fabric yields 11 yards of bias strips of a finished width of 1". One-half yard of 60"-wide fabric yields 13 yards of bias strips. A 2"-wide strip will require double the amount calculated above. A 4"-wide strip will require four times that amount.

3. To cut the strips, see Bias Strips in the A to Z section, page 131.

4. On the sides of the panel, fold *up* ½" and steam press. Lay a bias strip along one long edge of the panel and piece it to get the correct length, making sure a piecing seam line does not fall within 2" of the corner, because the seam will interfere with the mitering of the corner. Repeat for the other three sides. Fold under ¼" along both long edges of the each bias band and steam press.

5. With the wrong side of the band along the right side of the panel, pin the outer edge of the band to the edge of the panel, leaving 2" free on either side of the corners. Pin the inner fold of the bias band to the panel, and then topstitch both folds ¼" from the edge. To miter the corners, see page 136.

silk ribbon band with square corner

Silk satin ribbon is difficult to find, but you can create a band by cutting strips of silk satin fabric. The strips are cut from selvage edge to selvage edge, or across the grain, because the crosswise direction will yield longer strips than the lengthwise, unless you are buying more than one yard. Since good quality silk satin is costly, determine exactly how much you will need before you buy the fabric.

1. To determine the yardage of silk satin needed, measure the top and side of the panel and multiply by two. A finished 2" folded band requires a 4½" wide strip. Prepare the silk following the instructions in Getting Started, page 84. Be sure to even off the fabric carefully, as the line you create will become the cutting line for all the strips.

2. Fold the strip with right sides together and bring the long edges together. Secure the edges every few inches with silk or dressmaker's

stitching silk ribbon band

pins. Lightly steam press the folded edge, using a pressing cloth; do not steam press over a pin.

3. Adjust the stitch regulator to 14–18 stitches per inch, increase the tension, and, using a #9 or very sheer sewing needle, sew a seam ¼" from the edge, reinforcing well at both ends.

4. To turn the ribbon, see Step 5 in the section on ruching, page 94. Steam press the strip flat so that the seam line forms one edge.

5. Working on the right side of the panel, fold the raw edges *up* ¼" and steam press. Pin the silk band to the right side of the panel, matching the folds at the edges. Pin both inner and outer edges of the band. Blind stitch both edges of the ribbon to the edges of the panel, leaving 2" unfinished at each corner.

6. To finish the raw edges of the ribbon at the corners, fold under ¼" and press the silk to meet the fold of the panel underneath and slip stitch the folds together.

finishing the sides without bands

The side edges of a panel can be finished with a hem that also finishes the edges of the casing at the same time.

1. If the side edges have been folded under and steam pressed, finish them with a blind-stitch hem. If they have not been folded and pressed, fold the raw edges under to the wrong side ½" and steam press.

2. Fold under another ½" inch and steam press, mitering the corners, page 136 . Blind stitch close to the inner folded edge or use iron-on fusing tape for a steamless edge.

handkerchief hem

A handkerchief hem is the recommended way to finish all four sides of sheers, fine lace, net, silk organza, or other very lightweight fabric; it creates a narrow border on all four sides of the panel.

1. Fold under ¼" to the wrong side on all four edges of the panel and steam press. Turn under ¼" again and steam miter the corners following the instructions on page 136.

2. Sew the hem by hand using a blind stitch. Iron-on fusing tape can also be used, but it must be cut to ¼" in width. Follow the instructions in Fused Hem, page 120.

sewing the bottom edge

While the bottom edges of sheers are usually finished with a narrow hem, opaque fabrics are best given a double folded 2" hem that provides extra weight and allows an extra 2" for lengthening, should the panels ever be used on another window.

1. Follow the instructions above for finishing the sides.

2. Fold under 2" on the bottom edge and steam press. Fold under another 2" and steam press. When scrimping, fold under ¼" along the bottom edge and steam press. Fold under another 1" to 2" and steam press.

3. Secure the hem with iron-on fusing tape or a blind stitch.

welted hem

The welted hem is a stylish alternative to traditional drapery weights and adds a luxuriously thick edge of trim to the bottom of a panel, making it look heavier and fuller. Because there are no curves to go around, it is not necessary to use bias strips to create the welting. However, bias trim looks especially

sewing the welting cord

handsome when trimming a stripe or plaid. For a substantial look choose welting cord that is ¾" or wider in diameter.

1. Cut a strip of fabric that is 2" wide and as long as the width of the panels plus 2" for finishing. Cut a strip of welting cord the same length.

2. With wrong sides together, fold the strip around the cord, matching up the raw edges, leaving a 1" tail at each end for finishing.

3. Install a zipper foot and sew the welting cord.

4. Sew welting to right side of bottom edge of panel, with all three raw edges together. Slip stitch lining over raw edges of welting. Tuck the tail of welting into the corner where the panel and lining are seamed, or where the side edges are folded back, where it will add additional body to the corner. Slip stitch to the seam on the inside before hemming the corners.

sewing a lined panel

Lining a panel gives any fabric extra body and a look of fullness while protecting it from the elements. Interlinings are used when additional weight and thickness are desired, either for reasons of style or to act as an environmental barrier.

A curtain lining is added to lightweight fabric to protect a fragile fiber, to give it extra body or render it opaque, or to allow both sides of a panel to be visible. Drapery lining is added to provide additional weight and thickness to the edges. Hems are double rolled and the lining is attached to an inside layer of hem, creating a seamless edge.

Linings are sewn to panels in the following ways: The two layers are treated as one for shirred panels, or when lining is being added to lightweight fabrics for extra substance. By laying the lining on the panel wrong sides together, you can follow instructions for sewing an unlined panel.

When a heading has box pleats, the lining and panel are treated separately, pleating first the panel and then the lining, before sewing them together. When a panel is attached to a rod with rings or ties, the sides of the lining and panel are sewn together and the heading edges are slip stitched together. When a panel has a casing or a faced heading, the lining is slip stitched to the folded edges of the sides and the finished heading of the panel.

curtain lining for unfinished heading

1. Measure the length and width of the unfinished panel and subtract 2" from both measurements. Cut a piece of lining to these dimensions.

2. With right sides together, pin one side of the lining to the fabirc and stitch, leaving the bottom 1½" of the lining unsewn. Pin and stitch the other side in the same way. The two fabrics will no longer lie flat, as the lining is 1" shorter on each side (Figure 1).

3. Turn the panel right side out and steam press the seam allowances toward the lining. Steam press the fold line of the fabric on both sides. Fold under the headings of both lining and fabric ½" and steam press.

FIGURE 1
sewing the sides of a curtain lining

FIGURE 2
sewing a curtain lining to an unfinished heading

FIGURE 3
sewing a curtain lining to a finished heading

4. Slip stitch the top folded edge of the lining to the panel (Figure 2).

curtain lining for finished heading

1. Measure the width of the unfinished panel and subtract 2". Measure the length of the panel from the bottom edge of the casing or facing to the unfinished hem and subtract 1½". Cut a piece of lining to these dimensions.

2. Fold under ½" along the top edge and sides of the lining and steam press. Pin the top edge to the edge of the facing or under the casing seamline. Fuse or blind stitch the folded edge to the fabric, leaving the last 1½" of the bottom edge of the lining unstitched (Figure 3).

hemming the bottom edge

Follow the instructions in Sewing the Bottom Edge, page 100. Fold the lining under ½" and steam press (Figure 4). Fold under panel again and pin across the bottom edge, pinning to the inner fold of the fabric. Slip stitch the folded edge of the lining to the fabric (Figure 5).

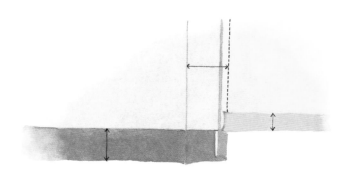

FIGURE 4
folding up the lining

FIGURE 5
hemming the bottom edge

drapery lining

1. Cut the lining ½" shorter than the unfinished width of the heading and 3" shorter than the drop. If piecing is necessary, see page 87.

2. On the bottom edge, fold under 1" of the lining to the wrong side and steam press.

3. Fold the bottom edge of the panel under 2" and steam press. Fold 2" again and steam press.

4. Place the panel wrong side up. Place the lining right side up on top of it and follow the instructions for sewing the sides and heading or sewing the sides with the finished heading above.

hemming the bottom edge

For extra weight, the top and side edges of the lining are tucked into the folds of the fabric when they are turned under to join the edge of the panel, and the bottom edge is folded double, creating four layers of fabric in the hem. Bands, tucks, trim, or welting can also be used to provide extra weight at the bottom.

The lined panel is hemmed last. As in dressmaking, fabric needs to fall for a few hours before it can be hemmed accurately, especially when several layers of fabric ~ panel, lining, and interlining ~ are used. Of course, if you are puddling, you need not be concerned with achieving a hem that meets the floor in a nice even line.

1. Fold under 2" on the bottom edge of the panel and steam press a crease along the bottom edge. Fold another 2" and steam press again. Fold the bottom edge of the lining under 1" and steam press a crease.

2. Follow instructions for sewing the curtain lining, page 101, folding the bottom edge on the creases and pinning but not sewing.

3. Hang the panel on the rod and let it fall for a few hours, then pin the double folds of hem to the panel. Stand back, see if any adjustment is needed, and pin so the bottom edge falls evenly.

4. Slip stitch the folded edge of the lining to the layer of panel underneath. The stitches will not show on the front side.

interlining

To add an interlining, cut it when you cut the lining, to the same dimensions. Baste diagonal stitches across both linings and treat them as one layer. Follow the instructions for the lined panel, above, to complete.

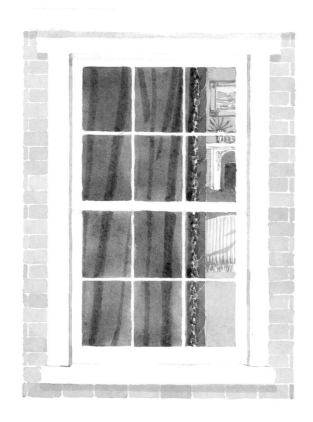

valance and swag

sewing a valance with a shaped bottom edge

Follow the instructions for measuring the drop and width of the valance, page 82, and sewing unlined and lined panels, pages 87–103, selecting the type of casings, amount of fullness in the heading, and other details to suit your needs. If you have to piece the valance in order to achieve the desired fullness, follow the directions for piecing on page 87, or see Railroadings, page 137. Seam lines can be hidden in one of the folds or concealed under a swag or tieback.

1. Determine how deep a convex curve you want at the inner edge. If the valance is being used alone, you might want it to fall to the sash or even to the sill for a dramatic effect. If the valance is being used with panels, hold a length of fabric to the window once the panels are hung, and raise and lower it to determine a drop that balances the window treatment as a whole. Also decide how narrow you want the valance to be in the center. Usually this is one fifth of the finished drop of the window treatment, but it can be longer if you like.

2. To determine the width of the valance, multiply the length of the rod by one and a half for a slightly gathered valance, by three for a shirred valance, and by four for a ruched valance.

3. When using a patterned fabric, the valance needs to be cut from selvage to selvage. When using a solid it can be railroaded (see page 137) or cut along the lengthwise grain, often eliminating the need to piece it in the middle. Fold the fabric in half so that the fold is at the center of the valance, and mark the fold at the narrowest measurement determined in Step 1, plus ½" for a seam allowance. Make another pencil mark at the deepest point on the outside edges, plus ½".

4. Draw a diagonal cutting line between the two points. It is not important that it be on the true diagonal, only that it be drawn straight across the fabric. Or you can curve the line, or make a scalloped edge.

5. Using the valance as a pattern, cut the lining to the same dimensions.

6. Sew the heading or casing of your choice following the instructions for sewing an unlined panel.

7. With right sides together, lay the lining over the valance and pin the raw edges together. Stitch the bottom and side edges, leaving the top edge open. Trim the seam allowances to ¼", clip the curved edge, and turn. Steam press the seam line flat. Fold under the seam allowance at the top, steam press, and slip stitch.

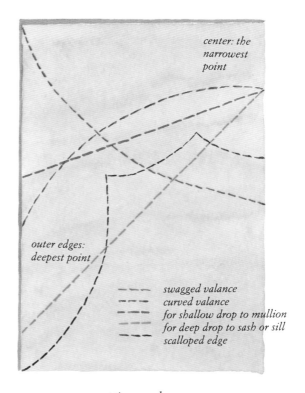

center: the narrowest point

outer edges: deepest point

- – – – swagged valance
- – – – curved valance
  for shallow drop to mullion
- – – – for deep drop to sash or sill
  scalloped edge

cutting a valance

sewing a swagged valance

Swags differ from valances in construction. Valances have a casing or heading and their own rod; swags are simply draped over the panel or curtain rod, or over swag holders or finials at the top corners of the window.

Where shaped valances create a concave angle, swags create a convex angle, their deepest point at the center of the window. Swags can be secured at the corners of the windows by encircling the valance with a tieback or threading it through a swag holder. Or they can be draped over a rod or finials.

A swag can be draped over a window in several ways; it can be folded over the rod, covering it completely, or attached to the rod with a swag holder. At its shortest it is a swag and tail, at its longest it can become a single panel that descends to the floor. The wider your fabric, the deeper the curve of the folds on the diagonal edge.

The short edges of the swag can be cut straight across or diagonally to become the tails, the part that hangs vertically below the swag holder or tieback.

1. For a swag with a tail cut straight across, determine how far down from the swag you want the tail to fall ~ to the mullion, sash, or sill. Multiply the measurement by two and add 1" for a hem.

2. For a swag with a diagonal tail, determine how much of a diagonal you wish. The inner edge of the tail can begin at the swag level or a few inches below, and the outer edge can be as much as 20" deeper.

3. Measure the width of the window and add it to the longest measurement determined in Step 1 or Step 2.

4. The drop of a swag is determined by the amount of fabric that is allowed to droop between the swag holders. We recommend that the swag be the width of the fabric from selvage to selvage.

5. Cut a piece of fabric as wide as the yardage and as long as the measurement determined in Step 3. For a diagonal swag, follow Step 3 for the shaped valance. If the fabric is light in weight, cut a lining to the same dimensions and sew it to the fabric along all four edges, leaving 4" open. Trim the seams, turn right side out, and steam press. Slip stich the opening closed.

sewing tiebacks

Tiebacks and swags require very small amounts of fabric, making them the perfect place to use a scrap of very luxurious cloth or needlework that is too small to be used as a valance or panel. For a matching tieback, yardage can usually be cut from scraps. A small ring, stitched to each end of the tieback and hooked over a small nail in the window frame or wall, holds it in place.

fabric band

Panels can be held back with bands of fabric, from narrow to wide, and as much as a yard or two long if the band is attached to the rod rather than mid-window. The fabric band can match or contrast the panel. You will need two small plastic rings to attach the tieback to the wall.

1. Hang the panel. Hold one end of a tape measure at the point where you want the tieback to be attached, encircle the panel, and drape the tape measure the way you want the tieback to fall. Note the length and add 2" for attaching.

2. Decide how wide you want the finished band to be, from 1" to as much as 8" (any wider and it will look cumbersome). Double that figure and add 1" for a seam.

3. For each panel cut the fabric to the dimensions determined above. If you want a stiffened tieback, steam press a piece of iron-on interfacing on the wrong side of the strip before sewing.

4. Fold the fabric strip in half with right sides together and stitch ½" from the edge along the long edges. Leave the short edges unsewn. Turn and fold so the seam allowance runs down the center. This will be the underside of the band. Flatten the folds with your fingers but do not steam press.

5. Fold under 1" at the ends and slip stitch the folds together. Sew a small ring to each end.

6. If the tieback is to be hung over the rod or attached to a swag holder, insert the raw edges of one of the ends 1" inside the other end. Fold the raw edges of this end under ½" and slip-stitch the fold to the fabric.

ruched band

Ruched or very tightly gathered bands are also called caterpillar tiebacks. To make a ruched tieback with shirring tape, make a band four times the desired finished length, and follow the instructions for machine shirring on page 88, stitching the shirring tape to the wrong side of the finished band.

To make a ruched band with gathering stitches, make a band at least 4" wide and four times the finished length.

1. Adjust the sewing machine selector to the loosest stitch. Sew the first row of stitches ¼" from the folds, and each subsequent row ¼" in from the last.

2. Carefully pull the top threads of each row of stitches until the band is tightly gathered, then knot the threads and cut the excess.

3. To finish the edges, follow the instructions for the fabric band.

tieback bow

To make a fabric band that you can tie in a bow with tails, follow the instructions for a fabric band, adding an additional yard to the length. Sew a ring to the center of the band, attach it to the window, bring the two ends around the panel, and tie a bow. If you want diagonal tails, fold under ½" at one fold and 2" at the other fold. Press under with your fingers and slip stitch the folds.

french bow

This wide bow, made of three separate pieces, needs fabric with a bit of stiffness (iron a strip of interfacing onto lightweight fabric). A very generous bow can be made out of one yard of fabric, making even silk taffeta or other costly fabric a possibility.

1. To make the tails, cut a 20" by 36" piece of fabric. Fold it diagonally from corner to corner, steam press a cutting line, then cut it.

2. With right sides together, pin the two long edges together. One edge will be shorter than the other; disregard that for now. Sew a seam carefully, as one of the edges is on the straight of grain and the other on the bias, removing pins as you stitch (Figure 1). Turn right side out. Crease folds so the seam line is in the center of the band; this will be the wrong side. Trim the long edge even with the short one, fold under the raw edges ½", and slip stitch the folds together. Make a second tail the same way.

3. To make the bow, cut a 20" by 36" piece of fabric. If the fabric needs stiffening, cut a 10" by 36" piece of interfacing and iron it on the wrong side. Fold the fabric in half wrong side up so the raw edges on the long sides meet in the center, and pin. Fold the short edges to the wrong side so they meet in the center forming a loop, and pin.

4. To make the band that will tie the bow and tails together, cut an 8" by 10" strip of fabric. With wrong side up, fold the long sides so they meet in the center.

5. To create the bow, overlap the narrow edges of the tails about 3" and place the bow loop right side up on top of them. Wrap the band around the bow securing the bow and the tails (Figure 2), remove the pins, and pull tight to secure. Slip stitch the bow to the fabric band.

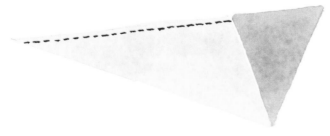

FIGURE 1

sewing the tails

FIGURE 2

tying the three sections together

diagonal stitched tieback

This simple tieback works especially well with lace and other open-weave fabrics but can also be used with lightweight unlined panels.

1. Hang the panel on the rod and determine the point where you want the inner edge of the diagonal stitching to begin, usually slightly above or below the midpoint. Mark the spot with a pin and remove the panel.

2. Mark the top edge of the diagonal line, at the casing or up to 6" below the casing. Using a yardstick as a guide, pin a stitching line between the markings.

3. Thread an embroidery needle with three long strands of embroidery thread in a color that matches the lace or open-weave fabric, or a double thickness of regular sewing thread for opaque fabric. Beginning at the lower end of the diagonal,

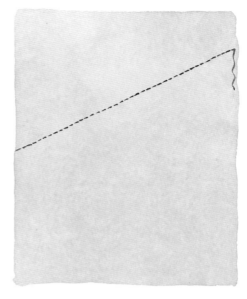

diagonal stitched tieback

sew a gathering line of small running stitches. Do not gather, but secure the needle at the high end.

4. Hang the panel and pull the stitching line until the tieback reaches the desired fullness. Reinforce the gathering stitches by making a few stitches, knot the thread, and cut off the excess.

silk rose tieback

The silk rose looks complicated to make but it is simply a folded strip of silk satin rolled and secured at the raw edges with a rubber band. You will need less than ¼ yard of silk, preferably bridal satin, to make two roses and a tieback band, and ½ yard of wired French ribbon to encircle the rose.

1. Cut a 4" by 12" strip of silk. Fold wrong sides together so the long edges meet. Pin but do not press the fold.

2. Tuck in the raw edges of one short end and begin folding the end tightly around itself. Continue rolling the band, removing pins as you go, until the entire strip is neatly rolled. Wind a small rubber band very tightly around the end with raw edges.

3. Cut a 4" by 8" strip of silk. With wrong sides together, fold in 1" on each short end and pin the long edges together. Stitch the pinned edge, gathering slightly between the stitches.

4. Lay the rosette on its side, roll the second band around it to form the outer petals, and pin in place. The band will go around the rosette more than once.

5. Stab stitch through the many layers of fabric around the rubber band, tightening the threads to form folds and and give shape to the petals.

6. Stitch the rose to one end of a fabric band, sewing through several layers of the rose. Wind the French ribbon around the rose, loosely crossing the ends under it, to form a nosegay around the flower.

cable cord and tassel

You can make a large drapery tassel for a fraction of the cost of a store-bought one. For each tassel you will need ¼ yard of twisted drapery fringe, preferable tricolor. For the tieback you will need a length of cable cord that matches either the fabric or the fringe.

1. Tightly wind one end of the fringe, and keep winding until it is in a tight roll, placing each round slightly below the woven edge of the previous round to form a curved top to the tassel. Stitch the end of the fringe to the tassel, inserting the needle through all the layers, and stitching back and forth to reinforce it. This will be the back of the tassel.

2. Untwist one of the twisted cords of the fringe until the double-folded cord is straight and smooth. Wrap the cord tightly around the woven tape, slip stitching the end on the back of the tassel. Untwist a second cord, preferably of a second color, and wind it below the first wrap of cord, but not quite so tightly. Slip stitch the end on the back of the tassel.

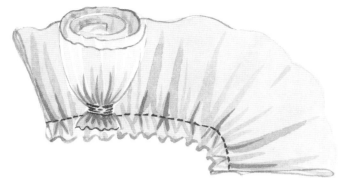

wrapping a silk rose

making a tassel

3. Fold the cable cord in half and slip-stitch the fold to the top of the tassel. Tie the other two ends and slip them over the rod or attach them to a nail in the wall, hiding the knot behind the panel.

CHAPTER FIVE

no-sew window treatments

Wonders can be wrought at a window with minimal sewing and common household fasteners like a glue gun, staple gun, pushpins, masking tape, or iron-on fusing tape. In no-sew window treatments, raw and selvage edges are tucked into or under a voluminous fold, out of sight, a double length of fabric is hung over a rod to become its own tieback or valance, or fabric is stapled, taped, or pinned to a mounting board. The secret to these treatments is extra yardage. Once you take this approach to no-sew treatments, creating them is easy, and the end result quite pleasing.

A reversible length of soft cotton is draped with simple grace over a rod and tieback holder, creating a Grecian look in an urban setting. The fabric is hung with very little fullness so it acts like a shade that filters light while screening out the public eye. The simplicity of the treatment, the fabric, and the coat hooks that hold the rod is contrasted by the use of antique finials and tieback holder. Pliable forms of lightweight cotton like batiste, gauze, lawn, or netting work best. Putting a thin fabric through the washer and drier will remove the sizing added to stiffen it, often improving its draping qualities.

draping

The art of draping, as old as ancient Greece, is a kind of sculpting in fabric, where gravity, not the sculptor, does the work. To achieve a fluid look you have to allow the fabric to fall freely to the floor and form its own folds, and then help shape the drape by pulling certain folds here and tucking others there.

To achieve the gracefully artless lines of the casually draped window treatment, allow extra fabric when measuring. This gives you the latitude to pull and tuck around swag and tieback holders to increase the depth and fullness, as well as to puddle an extra 2" to 12" of fabric on the floor. It is this extra fabric that helps create the look. All you have to do is make the necessary preparations, work with, not against, the body of the fabric, and then simply let the fabric fall.

draped valance and panels

The dramatic treatment of a single length of fabric shown on the following page is anything but timid, and is quite simple to do. Its deep valance will gracefully crown a tall expanse of window or unify more than one window treated together. The valance can be draped asymmetrically as in the following steps or symmetrically, with all the loops the same depth instead of varied.

1. To determine yardage for the panels, measure the drop from the rod to the floor following the measuring instructions in Getting Started, page 82. Multiply that sum by the number of panels you are making. This treatment can consist of two panels with a center valance (opposite page), or be completely asymmetrical with only one panel (above).

2. To determine yardage for the valance, measure the length of the rod and add approximately 36" for each loop you want to make, depending on the length of the rod and the depth of the valance. Traditionally the depth of the valance is the drop divided by five. However, this dramatic treatment requires at least a 12" drop or it will look too skimpy. Too deep a valance (below sash level) will make the treatment look too top-heavy. Although some loops will be deeper than others, allow one yard for each loop in determining yardage. To estimate the total number of loops, allow one loop for every 20" of rod. If the length of the rod is longer than 48" you will need to make an additional loop.

3. Prepare the fabric following the instructions in Getting Started, page 84. Do not cut the fabric. As you are working with many yards of fabric, it can quickly become unwieldy. To facilitate draping, fold the steam-pressed yardage back and forth in serpentine folds and lay the pile of folded fabric on the floor beneath the left side of the window (Figure 1).

The following steps for looping the fabric over the rod are meant to be a guide. Much of the success of this drape is a result of a combination of gravity and deep folds. Allow the fabric to form itself into lines and then refine, adjust, and tuck in the edges. If at any point you find your treatment varying from the instructions and you like the results, feel free to improvise.

4. Stand in front of the rod and work from the left side of the window. Take the top raw edge of the fabric and thread it over the rod from the back, pulling it down toward you. Holding the threading edge of the fabric in your hand, pull the fabric over the rod onto the floor, laying it in ser-

FIGURE 1
fabric placed in serpentine folds

pentine folds as before, and keep pulling fabric over the rod until the *other* raw edge of the length of cloth is touching the floor, with an additional 12" for puddling if desired. Laying the threading edge on top of the layers of folded cloth, pin the two layers of fabric together under the rod to hold the yardage for the panel in place while you drape the valance.

5. To make the first loop, take the threading edge and thread the fabric from the back over the front of the rod as you did in Step 4, and keep pulling the fabric to the floor until all but the valance has been pulled over the rod and the loop is the desired length (Figure 2).

6. To make the second loop, thread the fabric as you did in Step 5, this time taking the fabric from the front over the rod until the fold of the loop is twice as deep as that of the first loop.

7. Additional loops can be threaded in either direction. If you want both panels to fall from the back of the rod, you need to change the direction in which you loop the fabric over the rod. If it doesn't matter whether both panels fall from behind the rod, continue threading the edge of the fabric over the rod in the same direction as you made the first two loops. If you want to have both panels falling from behind the rod, create a third loop by threading the raw edges of the fabric over the rod from front to back. Pull the fabric over the rod until the loop is a few inches shorter than the second loop. This loop will produce folds in alternating directions.

8. Make a fourth loop that is slightly longer than the first loop, threading it in the direction you used in Step 7. If, due to the length of the rod, you want to make more than four loops, step back and decide whether the sequence of loops should dip again or become gradually smaller. The valance can

FIGURE 2
draping an assymmetrical valance and panel

go in either direction, as long as you stagger the depth of the individual loops ~ longer or shorter than the one before it, but not the same.

9. Leave enough fabric in the right panel so that it touches the floor at the same length as the left panel. Puddle both edges following the instructions for Grecian folds on page 114.

10. To finish the valance, gently slide the loops toward each other until the rod is completely covered. With your fingers accentuate the folds and ease lines so they flow into each other. Pull out the fabric tucked into a fold and distribute it to create more fullness, but don't disturb the overall flow of the lines that have formed. Fold back any exposed selvage edges and tuck them into the nearest fold.

pouf

pouf

A mainstay of traditional French window treatments, the pouf is both decorative and practical in that it can conceal a seam line or the point where the rod is attached to the wall. Extra fabric is pulled from the swag holder or tieback and then looped around the swag holder or the end of the rod.

grecian folds or puddling

The classicism of the Grecian fold makes it adaptable to a casual as well as a formal style. To create Grecian folds in any panel that falls to the floor, allow an extra 2" to 12" of fabric. The deeper the puddle, the more fullness in the folds, particularly in a panel that has been lined and interlined.

To form Grecian folds, hold the panel in both hands at a point 2' to 3' from the floor and move your hands wide apart to open the panel to its full width. Gently let go of the fabric, letting it drop to the floor by itself. Stand back and look at the overall effect. Where fabric is bunched together, pull it out

to create more fullness. Smooth fabric into areas where there is not enough fullness, but do not be overly concerned with symmetry. Gravity will have formed the overall drape in graceful lines. Rather than alter the shape, lift the fabric off the floor and let it fall again until you are pleased with the results.

bishop sleeve

A bishop sleeve is a deeply curved goblet-shaped tieback. Allow an extra 12" of fabric and use a tieback or swag holder that has an O or U shaped center, or hold the panel back with a loop of fabric.

To make a bishop sleeve, thread the panel through the center of the tieback holder, pull up about 12" of fabric, and let it fall. Arrange the folds for the greatest fullness. More fabric pulled up will create a sumptuous shape; less fabric pulled up will result in a gentle curve in the panel.

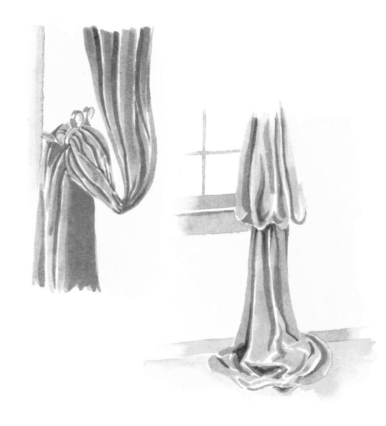

bishop sleeve

no sew headings and casings

self-knotted heading with cord

This simple attachment involves no sewing, works well with medium- to heavyweight fabric, and can be attached to an extended mounting board to cover an entire wall.

For this attachment you will need a pencil, medium-weight twine such as butcher's cord, a staple gun or hammer, and small finishing nails. For a temporary installation, use a staple gun so that holes are not made in the wall or molding. If the treatment is to be permanent, make but do not install an extended mounting board without hooks following the instructions on page 127.

Prepare and cut the panels following the instructions in Getting Started, pages 82–85. If you are using more than one panel, you can leave the sides unsewn and overlap the edges, or sew the sides together with ½" seams.

1. Beginning at a corner, make a small pencil mark along the heading every 12". If the last mark is more or less than 12" from the corner, make the last mark at the corner and adjust the next to the

FIGURE 1
self-knotted heading with cord

last mark, lengthening or shortening the distance between the two marks.

2. Beginning at a corner mark, grasp a bunch of fabric at a point 4" down from the raw edge and tie a 6" length of cord around it tightly to make an "ear" (Figure 1). The pencil mark will be visible at the tip of the ear.

3. Bunch and tie at the next pencil mark following Step 2. Note that this ear is twice as full as the first, which is only half an ear. Bunch and tie at each pencil mark along the heading.

4. Beginning at one corner, tack the ears to the window frame, extended mounting board, or wall, stapling or nailing directly below the knot where the attachment won't show. If you have more than one panel, overlap the corner half ears to make a single full ear, tacking through both layers of fabric.

5. To finish, fold under the raw edges of fabric between the knots. Fold back the ears of fabric around the nail and tuck them into one of the tight folds around the knot. Fold under the selvage edges on the sides of the panel.

casing with self-knotted loops

The knotted loop creates a series of graceful ripples that widen as they fall to the floor, especially with lightweight fabric that is also soft, like batiste or sea island cotton. Prepare the fabric following the instructions in Getting Started, page 84. Leave the heading edge unfinished.

FIGURE 1
self-knotted loop

1. Take one of the corners of the heading, grasping the fabric in your left hand about 12" down from the edge. Make a loop and tie it in a loose knot. Slip the loop onto the rod and adjust until the loop is snug but can be slipped off the rod easily.

2. Take the loop off the rod and tighten the tie. Tuck the tail end of the tie behind the knot and secure the knot by tugging on the tail and looping it around the knot a second time. (Figure 1). Tie a similar loop on the other corner, and treat additional panels in the same way. Thread the rod through the loops, and arrange according to desired fullness.

self-valance

This casing works only with fabric that is the same on both sides. Finish the raw edge that will be the edge of the valance with a fused hem, page 120, or by fringing the fabric, page 135.

Bring the finished edge up over the rod from the back and down to the desired length of the valance, usually about one fifth of the panel drop. Smooth the fabric across the length of the rod, then arrange the rest of the panel.

wire-threaded heading

Lace tablecloths, dresser scarves, and other handwork often have a design feature on all four edges that needs to be left intact when they are to be used for a window treatment. If you are working with lace sold by the yard, you can fold over the top raw edge and finish it with lace trim (see glued hem on page 120). You can create a heading for these by threading a thin wire across the lace ½" below the top edge. You will need wire cutters or an old pair of scissors, a length of single-strand picture-frame wire (the

braided kind will get caught in the openwork) that is 12" longer than the heading, and two cup hooks.

1. Bend back one edge of the wire to form a blunt edge that will work like a tapestry needle. Beginning at the top right edge of the heading, insert the wire needle into the cloth from the wrong side (Figure 1) and weave the needle through the openwork making tiny running stitches.

2. Bring the wire through the stitches and draw up a few inches of wire. Continue stitching across the heading, leaving 6" of wire extending beyond the beginning edge of the fabric.

3. Gather the fabric, pulling it along the wire toward the center, more tightly than you plan to gather it on the window.

4. Install the wire by winding its two ends around the cup hooks. Adjust the gathers, bringing the fabric close to the hooks. Tighten the wire by screwing in the cup hooks away from the window one or two turns each until the wire is taut.

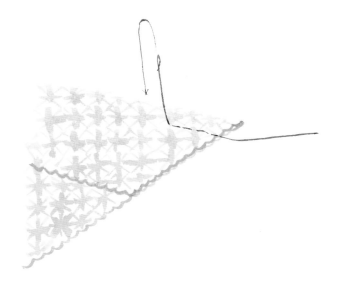

FIGURE 1
wire-threaded heading

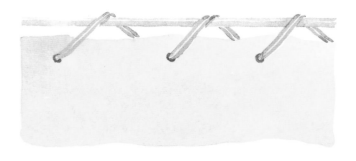 

grommets and buttonholes with ties

grommets and buttonholes with ties

Fabric shower curtains often make beautiful no-sew window treatments and have ready-made grommets or buttonholes along the heading through which you can thread cord, ribbon, or other trim. Metal grommets can also be purchased at a notions counter; tap them into a heading with a small hammer.

taping

Taping is a wonderfully simple no-sew way to attach fabric to a rod, to a mounting board, or directly to the top edge of a window frame. Use 2"-wide masking tape for medium- and lightweight fabrics and duct tape for heavier fabric.

taping to the window frame

1. With the fabric on the floor or a table, lay the heading *wrong* side up and create fullness by gathering up the fabric in folds until it equals the width of the window. Do not be concerned with making the folds symmetrical. Asymmetry will produce a better looking panel.

2. Roll the tape across the folds from one end to the other, leaving excess tape at both sides. Apply a second layer of tape to the edge of the heading so that half the tape is on the fabric and half on the floor or table.

3. Carefully pull the panel from the floor or table. Flip the panel to the right side and attach the 1" strip of exposed tape to the top of the window frame, securing the tails of tape at each end down the side of the frame. The fabric will cascade over the top of the frame and the tape will not show. When treatment is in place, trim off the excess tape that extends down the side of the window frame.

taping to a rod

1. Lay the rod on a surface and place the heading *right* side up on top of it, gathering it in folds as in Step 1, opposite, for taping a panel to a window frame.

2. Follow Step 2 for taping to a frame, securing the top edge of the tape to the rod rather than to the floor.

3. Roll the rod around the fabric until the tape is covered with fabric. Attach the rod to the brackets.

taping to a mounting board

Prepare the mounting board following the instructions on page 127, eliminating the brackets.

1. Lay the mounting board on a table or floor. Lay the heading *right* side up on the mounting board and create fullness following the instructions in Step 1 for taping to a window frame.

2. Secure the edge of the masking tape to the bottom side of the mounting board and tape tightly over the folds, securing tape on the other side.

taping to a mounting board

3. Flip the mounting board so the fabric cascades over the top edge. Secure the mounting board to the window frame following the instructions in Mounting Board, page 127.

no-sew sides and hems

You can secure side edges and hems and attach trim on no-sew window treatments with iron-on fusing tape or a glue gun.

fused organdy border with mitered corners

To make a completely seamless curtain border of 3½" wide strips, you will need a yard or two of 36" wide organdy and a roll of iron-on fusing tape.

1. Measure the length and width of the unfinished panel; you will need two 4"-wide strips of organdy the width of the panel plus 2" and two strips the length of the panel plus 2".

2. Turn under a ¼" hem on the long edges of the four bands and steam press. Be accurate, because the seam allowances can be seen when the sun shines through the curtain.

3. Working on the right side of the panel, fold *up* ¼" along the raw edges and steam press. These raw edges will be concealed when the band is fused.

4. Pin the wrong side of the bands to the right side of the panels, matching folds at the edges (Figure 1). Pin both inner and outer edges of the bands.

5. Fuse all but the corners of the bands to the panel following instructions for using iron-on fusing tape on page 120.

6. To miter the corners, bring the two folds of the bands together on the diagonal (Figure 2) and steam press.

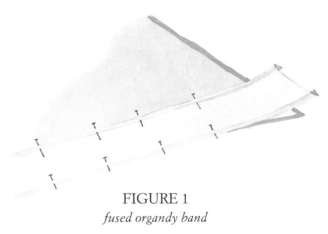

FIGURE 1
fused organdy band

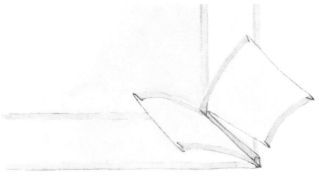

FIGURE 2
bands meeting at a corner

FIGURE 3
mitered corner

7. On each band cut away the excess fabric ¼" from the diagonal fold. Fold under this ¼" seam allowance and steam press. Lay a strip of fusing tape under the diagonal fold so it is underneath both folded edges and fuse with an iron (Figure 3).

fused hem

This hem requires no sewing, except for a reinforcing stitch or two in the corners. Fusing tape is an easy, quick, and inexpensive way to hem. Try it first on a scrap of your fabric.

1. Lay the curtain on the ironing board, wrong side up. Place fusing tape between the hem and the curtain.

2. Steam press the taped layers, taking care not to expose fusing tape to the surface of the iron, where it will melt. Keep the iron in one spot for 5 to 10 seconds. When working with silk, use a damp pressing cloth and a steam iron set on cotton. Satin finishes take extra time to fuse; keep the iron in one place for 10 to 15 seconds.

3. Check to see whether the tape is fused all along the seam, and steam press again in any spot that needs reinforcing.

glued hem

A glue gun is a quick way to attach lace and drapery-weight trim, especially multiple rows. However, the hardened dots of glue will show so for fine fabrics and sheers, use iron-on fusing tape. On any fabric use the glue sparingly.

1. Fold up the raw edge to be trimmed ¼" and steam press onto the right side of fabric; the trim will conceal this edge.

2. Heat the glue gun. Touch the tip of the gun to the fabric and make three or four dots 1" apart along the folded edge. Press the trim over the glue, using a table knife or metal spatula to hold it in place for a few seconds. Continue gluing a few inches at a time. At the ends, tuck under the raw edges of trim, dot with glue, and press.

fused hem

glued hem

no-sew tiebacks

Some beautiful tiebacks require no sewing, just some careful folding under of raw edges, and some tiebacks do not involve fabric at all. The following ways to tie back a panel do not require anything more than a few reinforcing stitches.

fabric band

To measure and cut the fabric, follow instructions in sewing a fabric band, page 106. Fold the raw edges of the long sides under to the wrong side until they meet in the center, becoming the underside of the band. Fold under the short edges 1" and tack them to the window frame or molding. Or sew a small plastic ring or paper clip at each end for attaching to a small nail.

braided tieback

The same folding under of raw edges can make a braided tieback without sewing. With one or two colors, cut three strips 3" wide and twice the length needed (see measuring for the fabric band, page 106). You can also use three long silk scarves. Fold the edges of the strips following the instructions above for the fabric band. Secure one end of the three strips with a rubber band. Make even plaits along the braid and secure the other end with a rubber band. To attach the tieback, remove one of the rubber bands and twist the other one around both ends of the braid, forming a loop. Hook one of the folds of the braid onto a nail, concealing the rubber band behind the panel.

self-looped tieback

The inside corner of a panel can become its own tieback if the fabric is reversible or lined. Simply tack the center edge of the panel to the wall or window frame and let the fabric fall gracefully.

self-knot tieback

Fabric can be tied in a self-knot in a wide variety of positions: high, at the midpoint, or near the bottom of a panel, allowed to fall to the center, or pulled to one side.

To tie a knot that falls in the center of the window treatment, loosely loop the fabric about 20" below the point where you want the knot to fall, and insert the lower edge through the loop. Tighten the knot and let it fall. To tie a knot that will become a tieback at the side, bunch the bottom edge together and pull the panel to the side. Then make a knot as before. Tug the folds above the knot to loosen up the lines of the folds.

hardware

Finials and swag holders make instant tiebacks that can become the finishing touch to a window treatment. Screw them into the window frame or wall, following the instructions in Attachments, page 122.

found objects

Let your imagination run wild and you will have dozens of ideas for distinctive no-sew tiebacks.

• Fringed scarves, table runners, table linens, doilies, and other pieces of fine needlework that are finished on all four sides can simply be tacked in place.

• A string of pearls, a belt looped around several times, ordinary twine or cable cord, lanyard, ribbon, a pair of baby booties on a ribbon, and any drapery trim finished on both edges make quick and easy tiebacks.

• For a seasonal or special occasion tieback, make a garland with a piece of florist's or picture-frame wire as a base for dried, paper, or fresh flowers and leaves. Encircle the panel with the wire and wind the ends around a nail tacked into the window frame or wall. Secure the stems of the flowers and greenery under the wire, twisting them so they don't show and tucking them into folds. Don't overdo it; these garlands look best when they are simple.

CHAPTER SIX

attachments

Simplified window treatments do not require complicated attachments. The only consideration here is fabric and the type of mount desired. Installation may not even require a trip to the hardware store. Rather than installing a traverse rod system for heavier-weight fabric, try two dowels and a pair of coat hooks. For lightweight panels, a pair of cup hooks and some wire can do the job in a minute. As an alternative to the elaborate cornice, a 1 x 3 from the lumberyard will extend both the length and the width of a treatment and increase the amount of light that flows into the room. If the hardware is to be visible, you can make a bold statement with decorative rods, finials, swags, or tieback holders. And searching for vintage hardware and found objects becomes a satisfying quest, as they can finish off your window treatment with a flourish.

The approach to hardware, from minimum to maximum, is the same: whatever holds up the weight of the fabric with the least effort and the most style is the best choice. Picture-hanging wire wound around cup hooks makes a virtually invisible inside mount and creates a floating effect for lightweight laces and sheers. Slender dowels or metal tension rods attach curtains in a recessed mount. In an outside mount, curved rods solve the problem of filling the gap between the rod and the wall and gracefully top off a treatment without a valance. Hardware for heavierweight fabric is often visible. Show it off to great advantage with decorative finials and beautifully fluted or finished rods. Mounting boards are used in lieu of cornices to heighten or extend a treatment to more than one window with a minimum of hardware.

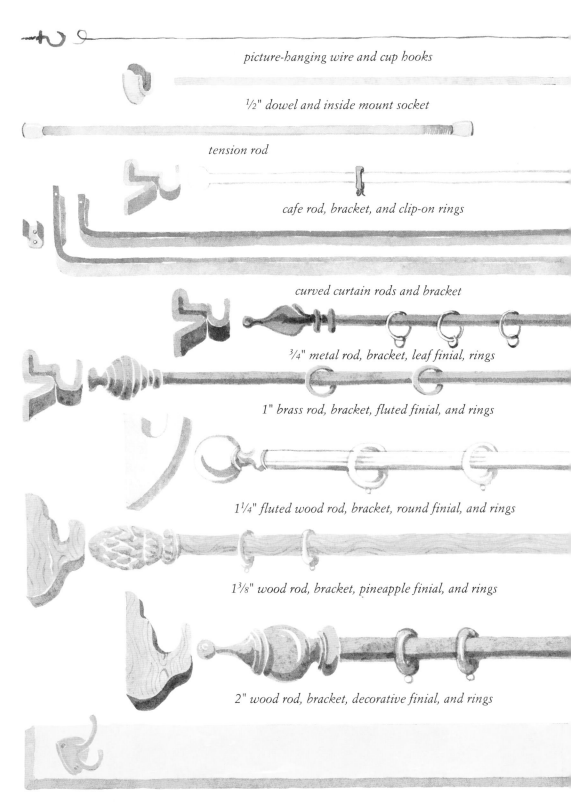

picture-hanging wire and cup hooks

½" dowel and inside mount socket

tension rod

cafe rod, bracket, and clip-on rings

curved curtain rods and bracket

¾" metal rod, bracket, leaf finial, rings

1" brass rod, bracket, fluted finial, and rings

1¼" fluted wood rod, bracket, round finial, and rings

1⅜" wood rod, bracket, pineapple finial, and rings

2" wood rod, bracket, decorative finial, and rings

mounting board with coat hook

hardware

A panel designed to open and close needs a rod ~ from as thin as a wire to as hefty as a 2"-thick drapery rod ~ and brackets with screws to attach the rod to the wall or window frame. The weight and fullness of the fabric and the thickness and length of the rod determine the type of brackets. The longer and more slender the rod, or the thicker and heavier the fabric, the more hardware needed to support it so it won't sag.

Rods need not be elegantly finished drapery hardware. They can be unfinished dowels from the lumberyard if they will be concealed by the fabric, a long slender piece of driftwood in an informal setting, or a length of single-strand picture-frame wire for sheers or lightweight needlework.

brackets

Brackets for slender rods and lightweight fabric are supported by a mounting attached with ½" screws. Heavier rods and drapery panels need the additional support of screws 1½" or longer drilled through the wall and into the vertical stud that supports the window frame, eliminating the need for bolts or plastic anchors in the wall itself.

There are two distinctly different kinds of brackets: one attached to the inside frame called recessed fixed or inside mount, and the other attached to the wall or face of the window frame called face fixed.

recessed bracket

Recessed brackets consist of a round bracket and a U-shaped bracket; you place one end of the rod in the round bracket first and then slide the other end into the U-shaped bracket. Although wood brackets are often more attractive, they are thin around the screw hole and can break under stress. Metal brackets are very sturdy and, once in place, hardly visible. Place the brackets ½" down from the top of the window for hanging curtains and sheers. Place cafe brackets at the desired level.

1. Position one of the brackets on the inside of the window frame and insert the rod to see whether it clears the inside of the frame. With a pencil mark the screw hole in the center of the bracket.

2. With a hammer and nail, tap a small hole at the pencil mark. Put the bracket back on so its hole is centered over the tapped hole and screw in place. Install the second bracket the same way.

3. Insert the rod into the bracket that has a circular opening, and slide the other end onto the bracket with the U-shaped opening.

face-fixed bracket

These brackets have two screws, one on each side of a hook or other U-shaped protrusion that allows the rod to rest an inch or more out from the wall or window frame. They range in size from very small metal brackets, attached to the frame for cafe and French door curtains, to extra-large wood brackets that support wide drapery rods.

The placement of face-fixed brackets is determined by both the kind of window treatment you are installing and the look you want. When you are hanging a single rod, place the brackets at the top of the window at the outer corners. To expose the plinth or other decorative molding at the corner, or to vertically expand the size of the window treatment, place the bracket on the wall, above the window and 1½" on either side of it. The bracket will be directly over the vertical corner stud of the window frame. To horizontally expand a window treatment, or for one that needs a lot of support, make a mounting board following the instructions on page 127.

When you have a window treatment that requires two rods, use the bracket placement described above for the rod that will hold the panels or valance. Install a second rod to hold sheers or curtains 1" to 2" below the first rod and 1" to 2" closer to the window on each side. These screws can be fixed into the wall because extra support is not needed.

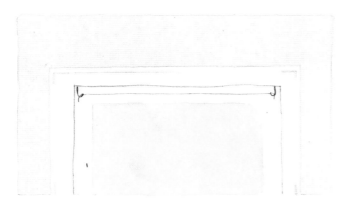

FIGURE 1

cup hooks and picture-hanging wire

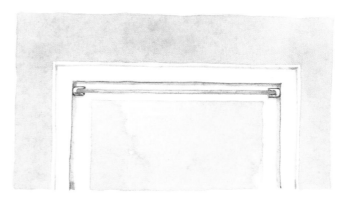

FIGURE 2

dowel and recessed brackets for inside mount

combined double rod bracket

You can also use a single bracket with two hooks, such as coat hooks, which will accommodate both rods in a single installation, the rod for sheers resting in the bottom U-shaped hook and the heavier drapery rod resting on top of the extended hook above it. This mounting provides an inch or more distance between the panels and the sheers, creating a cornice-like effect.

installing hardware

Each type of attachment, depending on the kind of window treatment used, has its own appropriate place and is installed with its own type of bracket or support.

cup hooks and wire

Lacy panels and sheers seem to float unsupported at a window when given the minimal attachment of two cup hooks and a strip of single-strand picture-frame wire (Figure 1). Screw the cup hooks into the soffit of a recessed window and wind wire around each one. When the curtain is in place, make the wire taut by turning the screw away from the window. Cup hooks can also be attached outside a window frame, and in extended window treatments. You will need additional hooks every few feet to support the wire and keep it from sagging.

inside mount

Hang light- to medium-weight fabric from a rod with brackets mounted inside the window frame (Figure 2). Insert the rod into a circular bracket at one end and into a U-shaped bracket at the other. The brackets can be metal or wood.

tension rod

A tension rod is the easiest attachment because it requires no bracket installation (Figure 3). A spring wire inside the telescoping rod extends it to the desired width; it is held in place by rubber knobs at each end. The tension supports light- to medium-weight fabric, but it may not be sufficient to support extra-full or lined panels.

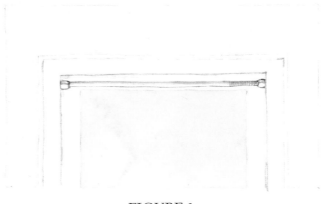

FIGURE 3

tension rod

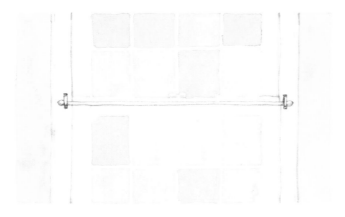

FIGURE 4
cafe rod with face-fixed brackets

FIGURE 5
curved curtain rod

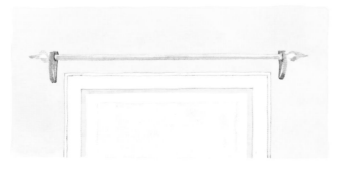

FIGURE 6
wooden rod, finials, and brackets

FIGURE 7
tiebacks used as brackets

cafe rod

Face-fixed brackets attached to the face of the window frame support a cafe rod in an outside mount (Figure 4). Secure the bracket into the wood with two small, thin screws. Cafe curtains on the inside of the frame can be hung on a tension rod.

curved curtain rod

Attach a curved rod to the top of the window with its own brackets and screws (Figure 5). The curve treats the top of a window without the need for a valance, and solves the problem of the return, the space between the rod and the wall. Extend the curtain rod several inches beyond the window on each side to allow for stacking space if the panels are very full.

rod and bracket

Drapes are often hung above sheers on a separate rod (Figure 6). Attach the bracket for the drapery rod a few inches to either side of the bracket and rod underneath that is to be used for the sheers. Brackets for heavyweight drapery need additional support and must be screwed into the vertical corner stud that is part of the window framework.

tieback holders used as brackets

For a decorative look when the rod and brackets are not only visible but are part of the design of the window treatment, use tieback holders, which come in a great variety of sizes, shapes and materials, as brackets on which the rod rests (Figure 7).

mounting board

Install a mounting board when you want to extend a window treatment vertically and, especially, horizontally. The mounting board is attached to the vertical stud of the window frame rather than the wall (Figure 8). This eliminates the need for molly bolts, plastic anchors and other supports needed for a wall mounting. A mounting board can treat more than one window, or an entire wall from corner to corner (Figure 9).

making a mounting board

Mounting boards are simple to make. Use a strip of 1x3 lumber for a single rod installation or 1x4 lumber for a double rod; you can add a piece of decorative molding to the top edge.

1. For the length of the board, measure the extended window treatment from right to left and add 4".

2. With a pencil, draw a vertical line 1" in from either end. Mark two screw holes along this line on each side. Place the mounting board above the window so that the ends extend equally beyond the window. Drill the holes with an electric drill, through the board and into the wall. Remove the board.

3. If masking tape is going to attach the fabric, you do not need brackets. All other window

FIGURE 8
mounting board with coat hooks

treatments require brackets. Install them at each edge, following the instructions for the face-fixed bracket, page 124.

4. Screw the mounting board into the wall, using 1½" to 2" wallboard screws, anchoring them into the vertical stud of the window frame.

5. Most mounting boards will not show because they will be hidden by the rods and fabric. However, when a mounting board will be exposed it can be finished by painting it the same color as the wall or molding, staining it to match the molding, or covering it with fabric to match the panels.

corner-to-corner mounting board

A mounting board or series of mounting boards can extend across an entire room, solving the

FIGURE 9
corner-to-corner mounting board with decorative molding

problem of how to hang a valance across the area of wall between the windows. In the case of a full-wall mounting board, measure the wall from corner to corner. When covering a distance greater than 10', install two mounting boards end to end. If a cup hook and wire mounting is used across an extended mounting board, install cup hooks every 4' to 6' to keep the wire from sagging. A thin strip of molding that matches the rest in the room can be attached to the top of the mounting board as an added distinctive touch.

decorative hardware

Like trim, the beautiful finishing touch of metal, wood, or glass hardware has a practical origin ~ to conceal an unfinished edge or seam. Many a

which might be too bulky to be threaded. The latter creates a graceful cascade of folds when sheers and light-weight curtains are passed through it.

Tiebacks usually have a decorative front and a bracket that is attached to the wall. Fabric is draped in the space between the decorative part and the bracket, concealing the attachment.

Vintage decorative hardware is much more readily available than vintage fabric, for the obvious reason that hardware is sturdier. In days gone by it was fashionable to embellish a window treatment with highly decorative hardware, from the sublimely simple to the highly baroque. With a plain, neutral-

decorative finials

color fabric, decorative hardware can make a truly dramatic statement.

stunning finial hides the sawed off end of a dowel, and swag holders are ideal for concealing the line of a seam in a pieced swag. Finials can also serve as tiebacks; the embedded screw can be attached to the window frame or adjoining wall as well as into the end of a rod.

Swag holders are constructed in two ways ~ an open U-shape over which fabric is draped, and a circular shape through which fabric is threaded. The former will accommodate heavy or very full fabric

attaching finials

Decorative finials are the perfect cover-up for the raw ends of dowels. They can also serve as swag holders. One edge of a traditional finial is flat and embedded with a screw, which is twisted into the end of the dowel. Many found objects such as baby blocks, a large seashell, or a fence finial can be attached this way, embedding a screw at the point where the shape of the object looks best when attached to the rod. You can also attach found

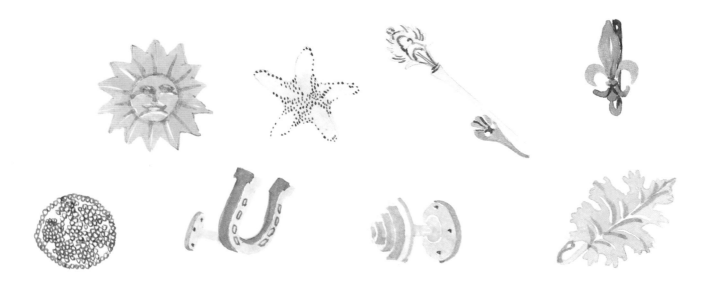

tieback holders

objects with super-strong glue, staples and staple gun, or wire. Because the finial is only decorative, the attachment does not have to support weight.

attaching tieback and swag holders

Attach the bracket part of these holders with fine wood screws into the molding around the window or the wall. As the holders do not support anywhere near the weight that the brackets for rods do, use small, slender screws to avoid damage to the molding or wall.

Install swag holders a few inches above and to the side of the corner of the window, or in the top center. Tieback holders are traditionally attached slightly above the midway point between rod and floor. However, you can place them high, low, and in between with great success, depending on the look you want. About the only place a tieback holder should not be placed is exactly halfway up the window treatment. A little above or below always looks better.

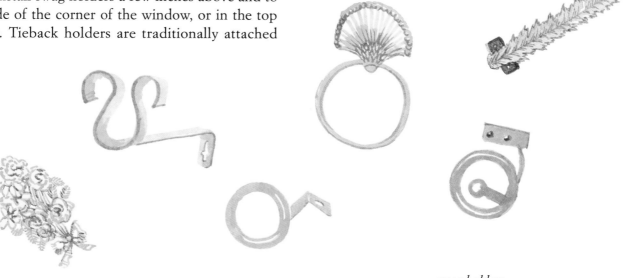

swag holders

CHAPTER SEVEN

terms and techniques A to Z

Throughout this volume, you will encounter numerous references to sewing terms and techniques, hardware, and parts of the window itself. Often, several words can describe the same item: folds of extra fabric that flow onto the floor are called Grecian folds as well as puddling. In such cases, one word was used throughout the text to eliminate confusion of terms. Here alternative words are cited in the following definitions. Precise terms for hardware are also given to help you select the right kind of brackets, dowels, hooks, and other items. For easy reference, the terms and techniques appear in alphabetical order.

apron

The decorative molding below the sill on a window frame.

bias

The bias runs diagonal to the lengthwise grain of the fabric.

bias strips

To the desired width of the band, add 1" for seam allowances. Prepare the fabric following the instructions in Getting Started, page 84. Be sure that the grain is straight before you proceed.

cutting the strips

1. Place the fabric right side up and make a diagonal fold (Figure 1). Cut along the fold. This is the true bias, and your guide for marking the cutting lines for bias strips.

2. With a yardstick and a pencil, mark parallel cutting lines from selvage to selvage according to the determined width (Figure 2). Cut out the strips.

3. Place the ends of two strips with the right sides together. Stitch them together on the diagonal with a ¼" seam (Figure 3). Steam press the seam allowance open. Repeat to create one long fabric strip.

attaching the strips

1. Lay a strip along a long edge of the panel. If a seam line falls within 2" of the corner, adjust the strip, because the seam will interfere with the mitering of the corner. Cut the strip even with the edge of the fabric. Do the same for all four sides.

2. Pin and then topstitch ¼" from the edge along both inner and outer edges. Trim the excess fabric at the diagonal corner fold to ¼" on each side. Press under and slip stitch the abutting diagonal folds closed.

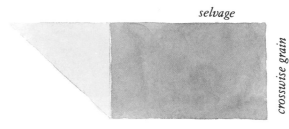

FIGURE 1

cutting bias strips

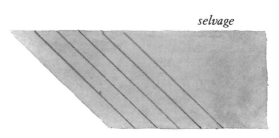

FIGURE 2

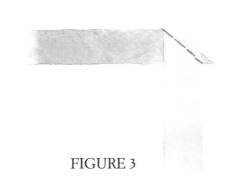

FIGURE 3

bishop sleeve

A deeply curved goblet-shaped arrangement is made on a panel at the tieback point. The flowing lines can be created by special hardware that has an O- or U-shaped center through which the fabric passes and is then caught up. An extra 12" is calculated into measurements for this treatment.

131

cafe curtain

blind stitch

Also called a hemstitch, a blind stitch is worked on the wrong side of the fabric and is barely visible from the right side. If the fabric is lined or faced it is not visible at all.

1. Turn up the hem according to the directions in your project.

2. With the wrong side of the fabric facing up, knot the thread and pull the needle up at the edge of the hem just in from the fold.

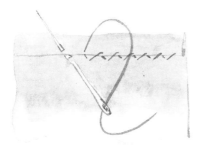

FIGURE 1
blind stitch

3. Take a small diagonal stitch, catching a few threads of the fabric underneath. Taking another small diagonal stitch, bring the needle up, close to the edge of the fold as before. Continue in this manner, spacing the stitches at ⅛" intervals (Figure 1).

cafe curtain

This window treatment covers the bottom of a window. Traditionally, cafes are hung on a rod at sash level, but they can also be hung at a mullion above the sash or anywhere in between.

casement

A casement window has two vertical sections that open outward on hinges, usually operated with a crank.

casing

A channel is created with two layers of fabric with parallel seams or a seam and a fold that run across the top of a panel, through which a rod is threaded.

clipping and trimming

Clipping and trimming fabric edges help seams lie flat, especially around corners and curves. To clip a convex curve, snip directly into the seam allowance with small, sharp-tipped scissors, cutting right up to the seam stitching, but not into it. To clip

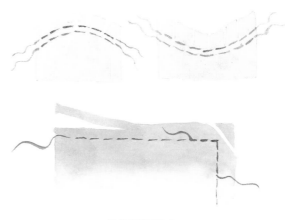

FIGURE 2
clipping and trimming

a concave curve, snip small triangular notches, clipping at 1" intervals and trimming to ¼". Corners are trimmed with a diagonal cut (Figure 2).

cornice

In this traditional window treatment a decorative wooden frame is attached to the top of a window. It is often shaped and covered with fabric.

curtain

A curtain is any panel of light- to medium-weight fabric, usually unlined, that can be drawn apart or closed on a rod. Although it can fall to the floor, it usually falls to the windowsill.

double fullness

A panel that is twice the width of the window creates this look. If a full look is desired, double fullness is recommended for medium- to heavyweight fabric and three times the fullness is recommended for sheers.

double-hung window

A window with two panes that can be slid up and down, double-hung windows are classic. See also sash, page 138.

dowel

A round of unfinished wood is used as a curtain or drapery rod. Dowels, which can be bought at 4' to 14' lengths and cut to size, range from ¼" to 3" in diameter and can be finished with paint, stain, or varnish, or covered with fabric.

drapery

A panel of medium- to heavyweight fabric hangs in loose folds to the floor. It is usually lined and/or interlined to create extra body.

draping

Draping is the art of creating graceful curves of fabric by looping it, tieing it back, or puddling the ends.

eyelets

A window treatment can be simply attached to a rod with a cord laced through a series of eyelets along the top of the panel. To lengthen the panel use longer cord. Lacing cord is sold along with other notions; ribbon or decorative cording also works.

1. Eyelets placed 4" apart along the heading will create generous folds when the panel is closed. Mark each point with a pencil dot.

2. With a small pair of sharp-tipped scissors, make tiny snips around each dot, cutting through the fabric section and facing, to make an opening the desired size.

3. Work around the edges of the opening with a buttonhole stitch, fanning the stitches around the curve (Figure 3). You can also use commercially made metal eyelets, tapping them together over the eyelet hole.

FIGURE 3
eyelet

4. Thread the cord or ribbon through the eyelets and tie it.

fabric

Fabric refers to the panel itself. Other kinds of cloth are referred to herein by their use ~ for example, lining, facing, interfacing, and trim.

facing

A facing is a strip of fabric used to finish a raw edge. Directions for facing appear in Sewing a Facing to a Heading, page 91.

finial

This decorative fixture, usually of wood or metal, conceals the end of a drapery rod. It often has a flat side with an embedded screw with which it can be attached to a wooden dowel. A finial can also serve as a swag holder. Found objects such as seashells or wooden blocks can serve as finials.

flat-felled seam

A flat-felled seam, which has a finished edge, is recommended for sheer and lightweight fabrics, and those fabrics prone to raveling. On the right side of the fabric the seam appears as two neat lines of parallel stitching.

1. Stitch the two fabric sections together with a normal seam and steam press the seam allowance open. With the wrong side of the fabric up, trim one side of the seam allowance to ⅛" (Figure 1).

2. Fold the raw edge of the untrimmed seam allowance under ⅛" and press (Figure 2).

3. Press the trimmed seam allowance toward the folded seam allowance (Figure 3).

4. Fold the folded edge over the trimmed edge and steam press flat. Topstitch along the edge of the fold (Figure 4).

FIGURE 1

FIGURE 2

FIGURE 3

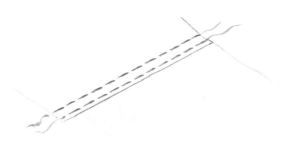

FIGURE 4

fringe

A decorative border is created by pulling out an inch or more of the weft threads that run from selvage to selvage, leaving behind a row of lengthwise threads (Figure 1).

Fringe can also be purchased by the yard. This type of trim consists of a woven band onto which threads, often twisted, are sewn closely together.

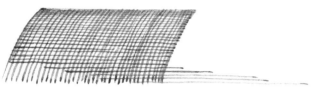

FIGURE 1
making a fringe

gathering

Gathering increases the fullness of a section of fabric by pulling thread tightly along handmade or long machine-made stitches (Figure 2). Gather panels without stitching by sewing a snug-fitting casing and gathering the fabric on the rod. See ruching, page 138.

FIGURE 2
gathering

grain

Fabric runs in two directions: the crosswise grain runs perpendicular to the selvages, and the lengthwise grain runs parallel to the selvages. The grain is straight when the crosswise and lengthwise grains meet at right angles.

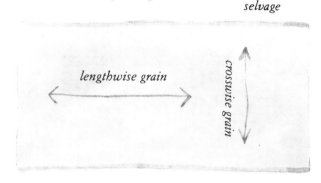

selvage

lengthwise grain

crosswise grain

grecian folds

Also called puddling, these are the loose, serpentine folds fabric naturally falls in when the panels extend a few inches onto the floor.

handkerchief hem

This is a double-folded hem that can be rolled or creased, and is mitered at the corners. It is used to finish sheers and other lightweight fabrics.

heading

The top edge of a panel or valance is attached to a rod with rings, fabric ties, tabs, or a casing. The heading is also the side that is gathered or pleated for extra fullness.

hemstitch

See blind stitch, page 132.

interfacing

Interfacing is nonwoven fabric that is sandwiched between the facing and the fabric to give shape and stability to the fabric.

interlining

Interlining is fabric that is cut to the dimensions of the lining and sandwiched between lining and panel to give extra body and weight to the panel. An old blanket, cut to size, can be used as heavyweight interlining.

jabot

A panel of any length, a jabot has a diagonally cut inner edge that is hung on its own rod, often under a swag. In traditional window treatments jabots are pleated, creating highly symmetrical folds on the diagonal edge that are accentuated with contrasting lining and/or trim. Instructions for sewing a valance, page 104, are for a modified jabot that is gathered rather than pleated.

knotting

Fabric can be knotted ~ folded over itself and tied, creating its own graceful folds ~ at the corners to form a fabric loop for attachment to a rod, or just below midway, or nearly all the way to the hem, to serve as a tieback.

self-knotted tieback

lining

Fabric is sewn to the wrong side of a panel, creating an additional layer that protects the panel from the elements, makes it opaque, and gives it extra body and fullness. Lining can also be decorative, its color a pleasing contrast to the fabric when the panel is draped so the lining is exposed.

mitered corner

Mitering creates a corner in which the side edges meet in a diagonal line. Steam pressing crease marks to guide you is the key to making a crisply mitered corner.

1. Place the panel wrong side up on the ironing board, fold up ½" along the edges and steam press flat. Fold up ½" again and steam press; unfold the fabric.

2. At the point where the second crease marks meet at the corner, fold the corner up and steam press flat.

3. Fold the edges on the first crease lines; cut off the triangle of fabric that extends above the folds. Fold up the edges along the second crease lines. Fuse or blindstitch the folds.

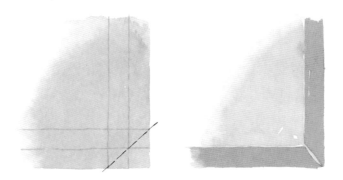

mitered corner

mounting board

A 1x3 or 1x4 strip of lumber onto which hardware for rods has been attached is then screwed into the wall above a window. (A 1x3 actually measures ¾" x 2¾" and a 1x4 is ¾" x 3¾".) The mounting board expands the height and/or width of the window treatment and also avoids attaching hardware to the window frame.

mullion

These are slender strips of wood or metal molding into which panes of glass are set. Valances, tails, and swags look best when they drop to the horizontal level of a mullion.

panel

Any part of a window treatment that falls beyond valance level, including cafes, curtains, sheers, and drapery, is considered a panel.

plinth

A square of decorative molding at the corners of a window frame serves to conceal the joining. Hardware attached inside the window frame allows the plinth to be seen. Hardware attached outside the outer corners of the plinth allows for a few inches of stacking space for the fabric to fall beyond the window when the curtain is open.

railroading

Sections of a window treatment are cut from fabric horizontally as well as vertically. Fabric that has no design or nap (surface texture), or that has a nondirectional design, can be railroaded. On fabric with a nap or with a directional design, the headings of the panels must all be cut in the same direction, and a valance must be cut in the same direction as the panels.

reinforcing

Stitching over an area strengthens it. When starting and ending a seam, it is necessary to reinforce it for a few stitches to make sure the thread doesn't ravel. Corners are also reinforced to strengthen the seam line before clipping and turning. To reinforce, stitch forward ½", reverse and stitch ½", then continue to stitch forward along the seamline. Unless otherwise indicated, all seams should begin and end in this manner.

repeat

A repeat is a pattern with a motif or motifs duplicated at exact intervals down the lengthwise grain of the yardage. Small pattern repeats can occur every few inches, but large pattern repeats can be as much as 12" to 24" or more apart. To calculate the repeat, measure the distance between identical features in the design. Although a repeat of a few inches will not require much extra fabric, large repeats can increase substantially the amount needed.

return

The area between the end of the rod and the wall is known as the return. It can be left exposed if decorative hardware is featured, or the hardware can be concealed by extending the last few inches of the panel heading around the end of the rod and securing it to the wall with a staple gun or small nail.

return

rings

Rings attach fabric to a rod. Washable plastic and brass rings are sewn into the heading permanantly; wooden rings can be sewn in but must be removed when the panel is cleaned.

ruching

Very tight gathers are called ruching. A tightly gathered treatment is made by drawing a very full panel with a snug-fitting casing onto a rod. A ruched tieback consists of two strips of tightly gathered fabric; also called a caterpillar tieback. The exposed part of a rod can be covered with ruching to complete the top of a window treatment.

running stitch

This is the simplest of hand stitches.

1. Knot the thread and, working with the fabric right side up, bring the needle up from the wrong side to secure.

2. Slide (or run) the needle through the fabric, taking two or three stitches at a time. Draw the thread through and repeat until you have completed the line of stitching.

sash

The middle of a window frame that has top and bottom sections that can be raised and lowered is the sash. A cafe curtain is often attached at sash level.

seam

This is the sewing line where two fabric sections are joined. If you are a beginner, it is a good idea to baste along the seam line before you stitch. Otherwise, use the pin-and-stitch method described below. Unless otherwise indicated, all seams are stitched ½" from the edge with the stitch length selector on your machine set at 12–14 stitches per inch (normal length) and the tension regulator set to normal.

1. Place the two sections to be joined right sides together. Pin, placing the pins perpendicular to the seam line with the heads to the right.

2. Stitch and reinforce at the beginning and end. Remove the pins as you sew.

seam allowance

The seam allowance is the amount of fabric used to make a seam and must be added into your calculations when cutting a panel. For window treatments the seam allowance is ½" unless otherwise indicated in specific projects. For example, to make a panel 48" wide you will need 49" of fabric, the additional 1" is for seam allowances of ½" on either side.

selvages

Selvages are the finished edges woven into fabric to keep it from raveling. Useful information such as repeat marks, fiber content, cleaning instructions, color swatches, a designer's name, and the word "colorfast" can often be found printed in these narrow borders.

sheer

A panel made of fabric that is transparent or translucent, sheers are available in natural and synthetic fibers.

sill

The sill is the bottom edge of a window; the horizontal molding that is the bottom of the frame.

slip stitch

Slip stitching secures two faced or folded section edges that may overlap or abut, such as the abutting diagonal edges of a mitered corner or the folded edge of a lining overlapping a welted seam.

1. For abutting edges, place the folds edge to edge and pin. Knot the thread and insert the needle under one of the folds. Take a small diagonal stitch and bring the needle up, close to the edge of the fold (Figure 1).

2. Take a small diagonal stitch, catching a few threads of the fabric underneath. Taking another small diagonal stitch, bring the needle up, close to the edge of the folds as before. Continue in this manner, spacing the stitches at ¼" intervals. Remove the pins.

FIGURE 1
abutting closure

FIGURE 2
overlapping closure

3. For overlapping sections, place the folded edge over the edge to be hidden until it overlaps the desired amount and pin. Knot the thread and insert the needle in one of the folds. Take a small diagonal stitch, and stitch as above (Figure 2).

soffit

The top underside of a recessed window holds hooks for a treatment inside a window frame.

stacking space

The area between the brackets of a rod and the edge of the window is the place where panels sit when they are pulled back.

steam press

If there is one secret to success in sewing window treatments, it is to follow the directions for steam pressing at every stage of assembly. Pressing open the seam allowance after a seam is stitched and pressing folded edges before they are hemmed ensures a flat, nicely defined line. Keep your ironing board, a good steam iron, spray mister, and damp pressing cloth handy.

swag

This length of fabric runs horizontally across the top of a window. A curved bottom edge is created when the fabric is caught up at the corners of the window and held in place with a band of fabric or a swag holder. Unlike a valance, a swag has no heading or casing; it is draped across the rod or through a holder.

swag holder

This is hardware or fabric attached to the window frame or wall; it has a loop or a hole through which fabric passes and is held in place to form a swag. Holders are usually placed at the corners and sometimes in the center. Tieback holders and swag holders can often be used interchangeably.

tabs and ties

Fabric loops sewn into the heading seam line of a panel that serve as attachments; the rod is threaded through the loops.

taping

Window treatments can be attached by taping the heading to a rod, window frame, or mounting board.

tassel

A tassle is an ornament consisting of equal-length cords hanging from a central knot.

tieback

Made of metal or fabric, a tieback encircles the panel and holds it to the side of a window, forming graceful diagonal lines.

tieback holder

This hardware, concealed or decorative, is used instead of fabric to drape a panel to the side of a window. These holders may also be attached to the top of the window treatment to support swags.

topstitching

This finishing stitch is sewn on the right side of the fabric, creating a narrow decorative border that shapes and defines the edges of a panel. Topstitching also provides additional reinforcement at the edges.

To topstitch around the edges, complete the panel to be sewn and steam press the edges flat, paying particular attention to the corners. Turn the fabric right side up and machine stitch a border of the desired width around the edges of the panel.

trim application

Whenever possible, decorative edges of braid, ribbon, cording, fringe, lace, and piping are stitched to a panel before the side seams are sewn, so that the ends of the trim can be incorporated into the seams. When this is not possible, the ends of any trim should start and finish in an unobtrusive place such as a bottom corner. In most cases, flat trim may be stitched along the edges by machine, but cording needs to be hand stitched.

An exception to trim application is welting cord, which is covered, then inserted between two layers of fabric and seamed.

general instructions

1. To attach trim to a finished panel, steam press the seam allowance or folded edge flat.

2. Turn the fabric right side up and pin the trim to the edge. Snip the ends, leaving a 1" tail at each end.

3. Stitch the trim in place. If you are working with cording, turn the fabric wrong side up. Insert a threaded needle through the seam line and catch a few threads of the underside of the trim. Slip stitch in this manner along the entire length of the seam.

4. Finish the tails, following one of the methods below.

flat finish

Any trim that is thin enough to be folded under without creating extra bulk can be finished in this manner.

1. When you stitch the trim, fold over the beginning end ½" and tuck under, securing as you stitch (Figure 1).

2. Trim the second tail to ½" and fold under until the two ends of the trim abut. Secure with slip stitching (Figure 2).

FIGURE 1

FIGURE 2

tucked finish

Some cloth trim is double- or two-sided, so that the ends can be finished by neatly tucking one into the other. Work on the right side of the fabric.

1. Fold the raw edge of one tail under ¼" and press in place with your fingers (Figure 3).

2. Insert the unfolded tail into the folded tail and slip stitch to secure (Figure 4).

3. On the wrong side of the fabric, stitch the gap in the seam line closed. Steam press.

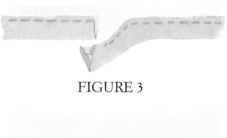

FIGURE 3

FIGURE 4

cording ends

Cording ends can be finished by neatly tucking them into a seam. Tape the ends of twisted cording when you cut them to prevent them from untwisting.

1. Snip a few stitches to make a small gap in the seam you are covering with the cord. Poke both 1" cording tails through to the wrong side (Figure 5).

2. Turn the fabric wrong side up, and slip stitch the two tails to secure (Figure 6). Stitch the seam closed, reinforcing over the cord. Trim the tails.

FIGURE 5

FIGURE 6

triple fullness

A panel that is three times the width of the window treatment has what is referred to as triple fullness. It is recommended that sheers be hung with triple fullness.

tucks

Tucking is a method for shortening a panel without changing the hemline. It is used in order to keep a decorative edge or border intact. For every 2" to be shortened, make a 1" tuck. You can also make deeper tucks, depending upon the amount that needs to be shortened. Adjust the amount of fabric to be taken up so you can make more than one tuck because two tucks look better than one, and three are best. Tucks will give drapery panels additional weight and give a neatly tailored finish to crisp fabrics like organdy or linen.

1. Make the first tuck so that its fold lies 1" above the bottom edge (Figure 1). Steam press the fold.

2. Make additional tucks above the first tuck, equidistant from each other. Steam press each fold. Sew each tuck ¼" below the top fold line.

FIGURE 1
sewing tucks

valance

A treatment that covers the top of the window, a valance works alone or with panels to conceal the headings. With an extended mounting board, it conceals the wall above the window frame. A valance has a heading or casing and is often hung on its own rod. Unlike a swag, which runs lengthwise across the window, a valance runs lengthwise down the window, and is treated in the sewing instructions like a panel with a very short drop .

velcro

Velcro strips, which consist of two tapes that adhere when pressed together, are an excellent way to attach a panel or valance to a mounting board. Velcro cannot be used for panels that open and close.

To attach the strips, secure one tape to the mounting board with a staple gun and slip stitch the second tape to the wrong side of the heading after the edges have been finished.

warp and weft

Threads that run the length of a fabric are the warp; they are crossed by the weft, which runs from selvage to selvage. When fringing the raw edge of a panel or valance, pull the weft threads out until the warp threads are as long as you want the fringe to be.

index